The Art of Saving your Soul
Through Prayer and Meditation

James Schreiner

Uriel Press

Copyright © 2022 James Schreiner.

All rights reserved. No part of this book may be used or reproduced by any means, graphic, electronic, or mechanical, including photocopying, recording, taping or by any information storage retrieval system without the written permission of the author except in the case of brief quotations embodied in critical articles and reviews.

This book is a work of non-fiction. Unless otherwise noted, the author and the publisher make no explicit guarantees as to the accuracy of the information contained in this book and in some cases, names of people and places have been altered to protect their privacy.

Uriel Press books may be ordered through booksellers or by contacting:

Uriel Press
1663 Liberty Drive
Bloomington, IN 47403
www.urielpress.com
844-752-3114

Because of the dynamic nature of the Internet, any web addresses or links contained in this book may have changed since publication and may no longer be valid. The views expressed in this work are solely those of the author and do not necessarily reflect the views of the publisher, and the publisher hereby disclaims any responsibility for them.

Any people depicted in stock imagery provided by Getty Images are models, and such images are being used for illustrative purposes only. Certain stock imagery © Getty Images.

ISBN: 979-8-8861-2010-3 (sc)
ISBN: 979-8-8861-2012-7 (hc)
ISBN: 979-8-8861-2011-0 (e)

Library of Congress Control Number: 2022914570

Print information available on the last page.

Urial Press rev. date: 8/23/2022

January 1

Happy New Year to all my morning prayer and meditation friends. Start the New Year with a fresh outlook on life by leaving old resentments, worries and anxieties behind. Begin with a new mindset, realizing how truly blessed you are. Know that God has a special plan for you. He will be with you no matter what your situation may be. Have faith that God's solution will be the best for all concerned. He knows your purpose in life, remember, He chose you for this assignment. You may have wounds to heal and old behaviors to unlearn. One of them will be to stay calm during all stressful endeavors. When asking God for guidance, creative abundance, peace and wisdom along with a grateful attitude, wish this for all your friends and family also. May this be a productive year for all. Know that better days are coming for your God is awesome and will give you the strength needed to carry you through any storm while helping you to grow and be happy. Be kind to others, stay humble and display a life of gratitude, making this an awesome New Year. Thank You Jesus

January 2

For this New Year I will lower my expectations of others by practicing patience. Therefore, I will lower my own anxieties and anger along with keeping higher expectations of myself to become a better person which in turn will raise my level of happiness. I will take a close look at my own capabilities and will set realistic goals for myself. I will take the action to change if my words or activities hurt others. I am going to choose to pause before I judge or criticize others, asking God to bless them instead. Rather than listening to the loud chatty monkey voice I will choose to follow my gut instincts. We will all be presented with different storms this year. If you have learned to remain calm during yours, teach others to do the same. May this new season bring love to your heart and bless you in many ways. TYJ

January 3

How good my day will be depends upon how I choose to view it. If I allow negativity to wallow around in my mind, I will have a negative day. Starting with morning prayer and meditation I choose to start my day with a positive attitude. Therefore, allowing me to make the choice to have an excellent day. When I align myself with God's will, I keep the door open to all possibilities. I will look at my day from a different point of view mentally, spiritually and financially. By doing God's work with a loving soul and staying on purpose, I will leave no room for the Darkside to fill my mind with fear or anxiety. Not everything I do today will turn out the way I thought it would. People may use me for their own benefit. What is important is that I do not lose my own identity by attempting to please everyone. Everything will work out just fine as long as I remember life is too short to hold grudges. The most important thing I can do today is to be around people who love me. TYJ

January 4

Joy comes to an unselfish person. When my life is filled with the blues, I ask myself, "am I all I thought about all day"? With morning prayer meditation God will say to you to "stop worrying, I will help you to plan a better day". He knows when you are exhausted and overwhelmed. God says, "Trust me, I will get you through this". Your power lies in how you choose to react to these situations. Rather than rationalizing and justifying your behavior and letting false vanity and conceit hold you back from finding true contentment; why not just express your regrets. He will make a way for all your conceived problems by boosting your creative thinking and enhancing your mental skills, allowing you to add a positive ending to your day. TYJ

January 5

As you defeat the Enemy from within there will be no room for personal judgement or hatred of yourself or others. You make the switch from critic to encourager. True happiness comes when you no longer need the approval of others for it is none of your business what they think of you. You receive the willingness to activate your blessings by thinking positive thoughts. With morning prayer and meditation, you fill that empty hole with tenderness as you grow in love and understanding. You replace thinking about doing a good intention with doing helpful deeds along with helping you to feel special about yourself, others and the world. You accomplish goals that are helpful to yourself and others. You find peace and contentment in the fact that God was and is always with you. TYJ

January 6

Patience and calmness will not come from thinking tolerance and tranquility at first. When impatience and anxiety raise their ugly heads, you must immediately counteract your fears and irritability with prayer asking God to remove them. After a while, this will become a natural way of life by helping resist the forces of Evil in your life and helping to refuse Temptation. When starting your morning with prayer and meditation you will begin your day on a positive note staying away from drama because of over thinking negative thoughts. With each new day, comes courage and understanding. Just for today, be kind to the person looking back at you from the mirror. Choose to be with people who have invested time helping you to grow spiritually. They are easy to spot for they are the ones who smile when they see you. Learn to respect the people you disagree with. TYJ

January 7

You have heard the phrase, "God does not give you more than you can handle." This is true if you seek God's help and guidance. You will run into problems when you try to do it on your own. Do not resist or fear change. Many times the other side of the coin is what you were praying for all along. There is nothing going on in your life that God will not help you with. All you have to do is start your day with morning prayer and meditation asking for help. You must learn to trust Him and never give up. It is important to be open and honest, for pretending that everything is fine stops anyone that God has sent to help you, from being able to do so. Stay away from negative people unless you are sure that God sent you to help them. Do not allow yourself to be used. Do not look back at your past in shame for it gave you the experience to be able to help others. May your emotional reactions be positive today. Happiness is about learning to love yourself, not from things out there. It is an inside job. TYJ

January 8

When facing life circumstances do I follow the Enemy's solution by making accusations and blaming others (victim) or do I seek God. I make the choice; Karma will serve out the rewards based on the good or the bad of my consequences. One choice I will make today is to practice the presence of God and rise above any tough situations in my life. I choose to stay away from manipulating and over thinking to solve my problems. My unhappiness or joy comes from my beliefs or opinions about any situation. If I choose to play the victim, the Enemy wins. When seeking God's guidance and protection, I win. I must make that same choice in every one of my state of affairs. It is when I chose to do morning prayer and meditation that I, with God's guidance, will then conquer my difficulties with ease. TYJ

January 9

Choose to make healthy choices when working, resting, giving and receiving. You deserve the good things that life has to offer. The Enemy wants you to think that you are alone and there is no one to help you. Stay strong for it is time to be happy and let things flow. Stay positive. Life's failures will keep you humble and success keeps you glowing. The hardest battle wages between what you know in your head and getting it to your heart so you can feel it. Remain teachable for you are not always right. Let go of the thinking that you can control others for you would first have to break their will to live. Not everyone is going to understand God's love, much less be capable of showing it. If "No" is a complete sentence, why am I compelled to rationalize and justify my behavior when saying it? TYJ

January 10

I must find my own truth. You finding your truth does not mean I will find mine. My change must come from within. With morning prayer and meditation, I will work on becoming a better person and not be afraid of change. I may lose a part of my personality and gain something better. Be careful of others putting on a big scene and pointing out how bad your life is and how you need to change. Do not allow them to control you. To diffuse the situation, tell them in a calm voice what you would like from them. Tonight, pray for those who hurt you and thank God for the change in you. The Soul's that have survived the hardest of times make the best Spiritual Advisors for they have been there and done that. They can help you to look back on your life as lessons to learn from, not with shame and regrets. You must learn to trust the person the Universe has sent to help you. TYJ

January 11

I find that not spending all my time trying to control others frees me to spend quality time with them. With morning prayer and meditation, I will grow with gratitude and want what is best for them. The most important person that needs to believe in you, is yourself. People may tarnish your image, but they can never take away your love of self and others and the good deeds you do for them. The people who really know you will always admire you. Take a break from others, to be alone, to appreciate and love yourself. An excellent Spiritual Advisor will have you focusing on your blessings, not your conjunction of events that caused your unhappiness. Through God's love you will stop thinking of yourself all the time and devote more time to helping others. When you take responsibility for your past actions, you will obtain the strength of mind to change. TYJ

January 12

You hold the key to the outcome of your life. It's called Karma. How you treat others will determine your fate in life. When someone does you wrong, do you forgive and give it to your Higher Power? Are you grateful for the people who made your life so much better? Are you aware that you do not have to have all the answers right now for they will come in God's time? Are you grateful for the life situations that made you wiser and stronger? Have you stopped hating yourself for who you were and started loving yourself for who you are today? My choice for today is to treat others with love and respect. That all my fears and anxieties disappear so I can be loved and blessed by my actions to motivate others to do acts of kindness. TYJ

January 13

If you are loving and kind on the inside, that is what you will project on the outside for you cannot get flowers from a sage bush. It is important that you learn to quiet that loud chatty monkey voice in your head so your Soul can gain control over your emotional outbursts. Your choice for today is, you can come up with 100 reasons to hate life and be angry at the world, or 100 reasons to be loving and kind. With morning prayer and meditation, you will have a better presentation of yourself. Find the courage to let go of what you don't know what his total plan is for you. You may have made bad choices in the past but each morning you will get a fresh start to improve yourself. Live a life that inspires you and others. Stop trying to impress them. TYJ

January 14

It was a painful lesson to learn that rage and resentments destroyed my inner calm and contentment for the only person being hurt was me. All I ever wanted was peace and tranquility. Once I find out that love conquers all and forgiveness is the cornerstone of being happy, joyous and free, my life changed immensely. Embrace your flaws, for they are the opposite of the principles you will live by. Work on them because they distract from and hinder your effectiveness. Know that you are awesome despite your blemishes. Once kind word can do wonders for others. You can choose to be nasty and hurt others because that is what cruel, emotionally sick people do. Make the choice to love yourself enough and to want to change to become more spiritual. TYJ

January 15

When feelings of discouragement arise, encourage others. How much of my life have I wasted because I was afraid to take a chance? Have I used people to hurt others? I will journal my actions to see what I need to do to improve my mental health. I have triggers that set me off. It is my responsibility to work on them so others do not have to tiptoe around me. With morning prayer and meditation, I will work on myself for that's who I will spend the rest of my life with rather than looking for the right person to be in a relationship with. Being happy doesn't mean I have everything I want. It means I am grateful for what I have. Seek God in the morning for He will afford you great wisdom throughout the day without criticizing you for any inadequacies. TYJ

January 16

When living for self my world is filled with fear and grief which in turn causes intolerance and strife. There is no peace. With morning prayer and meditation, I will know peace, self-control and love which in turn brings joy into my life. Every morning I am afforded the opportunity to become a better version of myself. I no longer worry if people are going to like me or not. I have plenty of friends who love and respect me. Today I have a heart free of sadness and my mind will no longer be imprisoned with worries. Instead, it will be a beautiful day full of God's blessings for He will guide me through any touch times I may have today. No matter how many times you give in to the temptations of the Dark Side, God will forgive and love you unconditionally. Let go of what you think your life is deemed to look like without any proof of self-knowledge. Make the choice to not try to fix anyone today. That is God's job. When your time on this Earth is completed and you go back to being a spiritual being, you will gain the knowledge that all your worries and anxieties did nothing to prevent it. Thank you Jesus.

January 17

You cannot allow outward circumstances to have the power to influence your command of thought. God did not create you to be depressed, angry or to feel unworthy. Worry destroys your inner peace and does not resolve tomorrow's problems. Everything happens in God's time, not yours. You cannot let material things, occurrences or others to be your first source of joy. Anger will punish you because of your perception that someone else wronged you. You put undue stress on yourself by trying to do it all on your own. Don't let you be the person who cannot see your own self-worth. There will be days when you must look at life's situations really hard to see any good and to stop worrying about what could go wrong. Positive people have a hard time being around negativity. With morning prayer and meditation and seeking God's guidance, you will be able to see the positive and enjoy God's benefits of life. TYJ

January 18

I pray that I may be open to the love that is being sent and deserving of what others have so freely given to me. I am right where I need to be today, doing everything to improve myself by doing God's will when completing the simplest of tasks, by helping others, with kindness, compassion and love. I exhale fear and anxiety. I inhale love and gratitude. May the light of the Universe shine through your darkest of times and relieve you of any pain and suffering. With morning prayer and meditation, focus on taking the action to change your negativity for by only talking about your problems you are living them. Let God do for you what you cannot do for yourself. TYJ

January 19

True peace of mind will come from looking at your own faults. Be glad God deals in Mercy and not justice. With morning prayer and meditation, you can have God in your life and will be able to let others find their own defects so they can turn them into principles to live by. Ask God to calm your mind and take away your worries by releasing stress and letting go of things you cannot control. You will feel protected by the love of God who sees all of us as treasures, not outcasts. Spend your time with God for He will convince you to believe in yourself so you can achieve your goals of becoming a better person. We each bring our own story into the battle of fighting the same enemy, The Dard Side. Learn to let go of your past, be grateful for today, and believe in a brighter tomorrow. TYJ

January 20

I feel the need to set boundaries in my life for behaviors I will not accept in myself and others are forever expanding. Others cannot fix me. I must quit feeling sorry for myself, by being a victim, and fix my own defects. No one can do it for me. I choose to rule my own mind, I will not let it rule me. Your thoughts become your actions so choose them wisely. Victims love to send others on guilt trips. If you don't want to produce the expedition, don't pack your bags. Hope is stronger than worries and anxiety for what I thought were my worst misfortunes turned out to be my best; for I learned my biggest lessons in life that made me who I am today. As I grew, in God's love, I realized He does expect me to change. I will be like the wildflowers. I will grow in areas no one thought I could. I won't worry about what others think about me. Some will question my judgement; others will doubt me. With God's guidance through morning prayer and medication, I will made choices I can live with. TYJ

January 21

I have lost the fear to change and stopped living in the past. I no longer put myself down and have quieted my over-thinking chattering monkey mind. When I am unhappy with myself, I tend to take it out on others. When I am at that point in my life, I do a gratitude list. I know I have healed from the past because I have stopped crying when I talk about it. Life is too short to argue and fight. Your EGO will cause you to do otherwise. With morning prayer and meditation, I have learned to trust in God's plan for me. I know my actions speak louder than my words. Talking isn't doing. If I don't take the action to change my words are totally meaningless. People will never forget how I treated them and how I made them feel. Don't judge me too harshly for if I do not see anything wrong with my actions, I will do nothing to change. Your part is to understand that you cannot fix me. The only thing you can do is to pray that I open my soul to want to change. Very simple but hard to implement. TYJ

January 22

People, places and things are not able to fill that hole in your soul for true peace comes from the inside, not from an outside source. God will always have your best interest at heart. Each person must find their own road to God. We cannot find it for them. We can be there for them to help find their God, as they understand Him. We can make suggestions so they aren't looking in the same old places and listening to the Loud Chatty Monkey voice of the Darkside; for their hardships from the past will make them stronger and their new life will be more rewarding than their past. It will start when they seek God through morning prayer and meditation. Remind them things will not happen in the order that they think it will. If they pray for a new house or car, God will not hand them one. He will give them a job to buy it for themselves. First, they may have to go to school to get a job that affords themselves enough money to pay for them. All in God's time. TYJ

January 23

There are negative situations going on in your life for a reason. God allows pain in your consciousness to get your attention. He wants you to seek His guidance. Take notice of these times of hardship and seek God's plan for you. Trust Him. The pain will persist until you have learned your lesson. God does not want you living in anger, sadness, fear or boredom. These are conditions of the human mind. Do not tolerate nonsense in your life. What is stressing you today will not be irrelevant next year. Move forward with morning prayer and meditation and God will raise your level of consciousness to a Spiritual Nature called a 6th sense. Do not let negativity affect you. Spend your time with people who have a positive outlook on life. Choose God's plan for you and not what others think you must do. It is our job to plant the seed, God does the watering. You cannot have a better tomorrow if you are still fretting over yesterday. Get over it, do the best you can today. TYJ

January 24

A good friend makes sure you feel positive about yourself and does not pretend to be a confident because they need something. Their actions will prove who they are, not their talking. Spend time with reliable, spiritual people who know you still have a long way to go and they are willing to make the trip with you for they are proud of what you have accomplished. They will help you to figure things out and to learn a new way of living by growing spiritually from the inside because they know that it is more important than gaining material things. Learn to show unexpected acts of kindness and change someone's life. You will lose the Darkside from within when you grow spiritually with God's grace. Learn to stop overthinking along with the need to understand everything that is going on in your life. Stop overreacting by learning, through morning prayer and meditation, how to respond to life situations. There is always something good in every day. All you need to do is look for it. TYJ

January 25

Be glad you are alive. Appreciate what you have. The most important thing you can do today is show kindness to others and gain the wisdom of how God's love really works. The best people are the ones that help you to feel loved and wanted. Today I will not compare myself to others. I will remain calm no matter what the Darkside throws at me today. God created me to be me, not someone else's version of who they think I should be. With morning prayer and meditation, seek God's guidance for he will install feelings of gratitude to help you to make it through the day. You are needed, loved and stronger than you think. You are alive because God is not finished with you. Be the Beautiful Soul God sees you as. TYJ

January 26

When the Darkside's voice is sending you thoughts of guilt and shame for your past wrongful deeds, substitute that negative voice with positive affirmations. He wants you to feel guilty and to give up on yourself. You can face your fears and overcome them by starting your morning with prayer and meditation. You will then be surrounded by love. Discipline your mind to make wiser choices and treat yourself and others with love and kindness. You will have good days and bad days. What is important is how you react to them. Don't allow yourself to get too high or too low. Stop with the excuses and justifications. Never give up and you will have a successful Journey. Choose to take the action to change therefore giving yourself the best gift you can by living your life to the fullest. Stop allowing that loud chatty monkey voice to have you looking for reasons that you are not good enough. Change is going to feel uncomfortable at first. Learn how to be alone without being lonely for self-love is the biggest gift you can give yourself. TYJ

January 27

A healthy body starts with a healthy mind. Staying annoyed by insults that others say or do to you is a choice and not a wise one at that. You will spend an enormous amount of time in your own head so be gentle on yourself. Know that starting your day with morning prayer and meditation you will be accomplishing the hardest things to do which usually turns out to be the best for you. Put in the effort and leave the outcome to God. You are showing great wisdom when you walk away from people who are bad for your emotional health. Do daily affirmations to unlearn unhealthy beliefs that you were taught from childhood by not allowing them to take up space in your head. Look within yourself and realize how capable you are. Things may look dark right now but know that better times are coming. Choose to make your life the best it can be, don't settle for mediocrity. By finding yourself, you will set your mind free to be who God meant you to be. Walk through that door that you were praying would open. TYJ

January 28

Serenity is having the Faith that God will carry you through any storms that are going on in your life until you can learn your lessons and then the good can happen in your life. You can close your eyes to what is going on in your life, but you cannot close your mind to what you don't want to feel. Don't wait for life to get better to improve your emotional state of mind for life can be complicated. Negativity is contagious so choose to be joyous, tell your story for it may help someone to survive. Do not judge others, help to heal those who are hurting emotionally. Pray, meditate, have an attitude of gratitude, rest, eat healthy, read something positive daily for you are worthy of God's unending love. The more you think you can handle any situation, the less power you give to God who can handle any circumstance. TYJ

January 29

Just for today I will not worry, judge or be critical of others. I will surround myself with solid people who love me unconditionally and will not let the problems of today steal my happiness. I will be grateful for my world today and vow to make it better. I have the faith that I will survive any bad that happens for it will be temporary and better days are on the way; since I can feel it in my soul where peace of mind will prevail despite the loud chatty Darkside. God has supplied you with everything you will need for Spiritual growth so all you need to do is let go of any negativity that is clouding your mind. Stop creating your own drama. TYJ

January 30

With morning prayer and meditation, I find that I receive the gifts of honesty, faith and the strength to face the Darkside. I have been given freedom from self-deception, the Faith to draw from a Higher Power and the ability to control my fears in difficult situations without reliance on mood-altering chemicals or material stuff from the outside. I am no longer impressed with social status or job titles. I look at how you treat others for anger given, anger received. Karma can be a bitch. Your choice. Stay strong. Never lose hope. May your Spiritual Journey help you to rid yourself of negativity and give you a loving Soul TYJ

January 31

Are you willing to evaluate your present condition truthfully? Will you let go of false pride and arrogance knowing only a relationship with your Higher Power will fill that big empty hole in your Soul? For true happiness you must let go of the past and those painful memories of your childhood that are deeply buried in your subconscious. You have fought battles, cried tears and been rejected but here you are today, a smiling humble person walking in the Sunlight of the Spirit. Your ability to help others has made you a beautiful child of God. Be cautious, the Darkside will never give up. He had control over you in the past, with addictions, and will continue fighting to get you back, to your life of disparity. You must resist Him. TYJ

February 1

Your biggest challenge will be the lack of presence of God in your life. Not all the people you meet are meant to stay in your life. They come to teach you a lesson. God and your family are meant to stay in your life forever. In morning prayer and meditation, start with having God in your life for 1 hour. A small contemplation can start a lifetime of peace and serenity. A negative product of thinking will keep you absorbed in fear and anxiety for what you create in your mind is what your life will exemplify. Your choice. Difficult times give you opportunities for Spiritual growth for they help to build strength and character along with teaching invaluable lessons. Do not complain during these circumstances that make it possible for growth. Opinions are like buttholes; everyone has got one. Be grateful for the blessings God has bestowed upon you by being an exceptional example of gentleness and kindness with yourself and others, for it makes you beautiful. TYJ

February 2

When living a life filled with anger and resentments, you cannot expect love and kindness to exist in your life. With morning prayer and meditation, empty yourself of the Darkside and allow the love of God to come into your life for God does not live in an angry house. Face the facts, make a true evaluation of your life, for only then will you have a chance at meekness. Ask God to help you, to be willing to practice forgiveness and develop your mind. Allow the silent voice of confidence to come into your life. Get rid of the loud chatty monkey voice of insecurities. Learn to face the truth and quit running back to your addictions. Cease inviting people, who you feel you need in your life by learning to live alone in solitude and by making the choice to heal from your broken past. Stop the negative self-put-downs by avoiding visiting your past mistakes. Just for today, count your blessings and live a life filled with gratitude and be finished with the idea that you are better than others. TYJ

February 3

Start your day with loving thoughts of yourself and others. Know that you are worthy of honesty and respect. Be thankful for the little things in your life. Go today without complaining and give yourself permission to heal. Your mind cannot be positive and negative at the same time. Pay attention to your thoughts because you see things as you are, not as your life really is. Every morning you get to choose stress or peace by which thought you bring into your mind. Your attitude will either bring you peace or stress. Feel good about yourself without needing the approval of others. Be grateful for the new you that has come from the problems you have had in the past. Remember God is stronger than any problem you may have or had. It is ok to have a good cry, just don't forget to get back up and be the person God meant you to be. Be strong and alive. Surround yourself with people who respect you and will help you keep all the promises you make. Go forward with the love of God and friends. TYJ

February 4

It is important to perceive when to let go of people who are harmful to your serenity. You do not have to hang with abusive people. That does not make you better than anyone else, just wiser. With morning prayer and meditation in your life, it is safe to step forward asking for what you want out of life. If you don't ask, the answer will always be no. along the same lines, if you don't see anything wrong with your life, it will never get better. Give yourself permission to alter your life. When you do make the choice to improve, affirm that your life will never go back to the old ways. Don't carry your faulty judgments around with you. Be aware that a lot of your actions were based on inadequate knowledge. Personal experience tells you that hurting people hurt others. If you want to be happy, you will have to let go of what is gone and look forward to the new you. Pray for the strength to endure any difficulties that may come your way. TYJ

February 5

Wishing to be someone else is poison. Awaken to your inner beauty. Realize your own uniqueness. Be who you are and bloom where you are planted. Learn to be happy today. Don't wait for things to get easier or better. Live your life with love, honesty, truth and respect. With morning prayer and meditation, your heavy loads will be lightened, and you will be given the strength to carry on when feelings of weakness overcome you. May today be filled with love, serenity and inner peace. You may have loved the wrong people and made bad choices in the past but living there can initiate depression. Projecting the future can cause anxiety. God always looks beyond your imperfections and sees only the good in you, so choose to stay in today and give yourself permission to have fun. TYJ

February 6

If you lost everything today, I pray that you still choose to have God in your life. Some days will be better than others, look for the best in your life. With morning prayer and meditation, you will stay strong, be positive and will invariably be at your best when treating others with love and kindness. The past is gone, have no fear of the future for by living in the present, you know that life is beautiful, although not perfect but a whole lot better than when you started this new journey in life. Thank God for the people who look beyond your imperfections, did not let you walk along and loved you when you were incapable of loving yourself. Self-love will be the most important achievement you can obtain in your life, for without it all the degrees and professional recognition will be meaningless. TYJ

February 7

Everything happens for a reason. If painful situations keep happening in your life, stop and look at them for God is relaying a message to work on yourself to relieve the pain and suffering. Stress can destroy your physical health, deplete your hope along with ruining your spirituality. Serenity is a byproduct of stopping your complaining about how bad your life is and being grateful for what you have. A negative mind cannot produce a positive life. Be proud of how far you have come for you have lived through some tough times therefore making you who you are today. Genuine honesty helps you to become trustworthy. You have come to love yourself enough to want to work on your defects. Seek God's help for only you can work on your non desirable characteristics. No other human being can fix them for you. God is working in your life so learn to trust Him. Out of your worst Darkness comes your greatest beauty, mentally strong courage and toughness. TYJ

February 8

Be leery of people who have a problem for every solution. Being ambitious and energetic still requires a plan to get anything accomplished. Morning prayer and meditation is an important part of a process to reach your goals. Earnestly ask for your friends to be blessed with good health, improved finances, that their worries and anxieties disappear, and they make peace with their past. Give them the knowledge to realize they don't have a monopoly on all of life's problems and the wisdom to know that they are never alone. God's choice for you and them is to be positive. Make your days count. Never underestimate the power of communicating with God, for peace and serenity starts with you. Please don't ruin the day for others just because you made the choice not to be positive. Instead, select to go with the flow of life and to be an inspiration for others. TYJ

February 9

Just for today, choose to set yourself free by deciding to forgive others because resentments make you bitter. Watch your tongue when your heart is full of anger. Never wish anyone bad luck or to have harm befall them. Instead, pray for them to receive God's healing power. Set healthy boundaries and stay away from people who lie to you, disrespect you, use you or put you down. Sometimes the only way to win is not to play. We don't need a lot of friends, just real ones. With morning prayer and meditation, make the choice to have a really great day and then go have one. Pray for others to make better choices in their lives, remembering that you are not responsible for others making bad ones. TYJ

February 10

Look at your life with gratitude in your heart for it is received from God's good grace and kindness. If someone in your life is saying they hate you or are angry with you, what they are saying is you hurt me. Look at your part. Their anger is a shield form the pain they are feeling. Ask for forgiveness for your part. You are not perfect. You have and will continue to make bad choices. Learn to get back up. With morning prayer and meditation, you will make better choices in the future. Wrong is wrong, stop rationalizing and justifying your behavior to fit in. Be yourself by learning to embrace your inner Light, taking your Power back and becoming involved in your recovery. When you know better, you must do better. TYJ

February 11

Ask God for help with all issues, gratifying or annoying. Have the courage to deal with the realities of life without the reliance of mood-altering chemicals or outside rewards. With strength of character, you can endure the things you cannot change. Be fearless in the practice of faith and in believing that your sorrows won't last forever. Never lose hope for miracles do happen. The less stress you have in your life the more peaceful it will become. If God woke you up today, then He will be with you through all things big or small. Just breathe and enjoy. He wants you to go make a difference in someone's life today. Be real and kind, along with projecting all the humility you can muster. Do not take the easier, softer way on all matters pertaining to your life, for God will be with you helping you to keep your life simple. He may not open any new doors today. Learn to pause, relax and praise Him for the good He has bestowed upon you. TYJ

February 12

You are not a perfect person. You make bad choices which leads to mistakes. With morning prayer and meditation, you can work on your lack of appreciation and that feeling of emptiness in your soul. One feeds into the other. Change starts from the inside. Adapt an attitude of gratitude for everything is a gift from God, yes even the bad. Stay strong through the bad times and God will give you reasons to smile. You are given the ability to learn from your mistakes. So, move on vowing to do better next time by making a conscious effort to bring God into your daily routine. Enlarge your capacity to give love and kindness to others. You transform your thinking from "do I have to do this?" to "I will gladly do this for you"; thus, changing your thinking from anxiety to blessings, gladly praying that everyone has their best day ever. TYJ

February 13

Do not wait for the other person to say the 2 hardest words, "I'm sorry." Starting with morning prayer and meditation, you can begin the healing process. Bring joy back into your life for happiness comes from doing the right things. Making amends keeps you humble and strong, demands courage and allows you to share your strength with someone else. God showed you Grace when He forgave you for your past wrongful deeds. The least you can do is take God's hand and walk with Him today. Life is too short to spend your time in bitterness. By finding tranquility within your soul, you can choose to be at peace with others and stop making their life difficult. You may have to look at documental proof that contradicts your way of seeing things and admit you may be wrong. Believe that God only wants what is best for you. Never take anything for granted. Everyday tell the people who are important to you, that you love them. TYJ

February 14

One small positive thought will change your day. Learn to appreciate what you have by being grateful for your life today. Believe in yourself, be patient, change takes time. You made the choice to leave your old life behind so let your Angels help and comfort you. With morning prayer and meditation, you can stop responding to life with your old perceptions and choose to practice peace and serenity by looking for the good so you can begin your new life with grace and ease. All the past pain and failures are what made you strong today so leave them there. Stop trying to open old doors that are locked. You were never meant to live a life of being ashamed, feeling guilty, suffering from depression or feeling unworthy. Each morning is a new beginning, ask God to create a masterpiece. Choose to not let anything upset you today so you can eliminate painful addictions from your life. This is the moment that will change you or keep you in misery. Your choice. Stop trying to impress or worry about another's opinion if their name is not God. TYJ

February 15

Acceptance is the key to transforming your life for the better. You can choose to be miserable or if you don't like the way your life is heading, you can break up with the past and alter your thinking by taking on a more positive attitude. Being critical and demanding is a pathway to loneliness. Modify your behavior and you will become different. Be kind to your own self for once you learn to respect you personally, you will earn it from others. Sometimes you act out because your EGO wants attention. If you are upset with someone, you need to talk to them, not about them. Remember true happiness comes from making the choice to do what is right, not what is comfortable or easy. Through morning prayer and meditation, you will be blessed with God's grace and favor and will truly enjoy showing love and kindness to others, even when their actions prove they don't deserve it. TYJ

February 16

With morning prayer and meditation, God will present you with opportunities for growth. By handling things on your own you will produce some bad days. You may end up uttering a victim's famous words; "why do people treat me so badly?" You are a product of your decisions. You must be careful of people whose actions don't match their words. Their activities prove who they are. You cannot control anyone's loyalty. Loving them to the end of time will not change them. All you can do is pray for them for only God can perform miracles. Until then, you may find it necessary to disconnect so you can find peace and serenity. You have an obligation to stop them from blaming you for everything bad going on in their life. Do not let the aforementioned make you feel inadequate. Breathing in God's love you will count your blessings, show kindness, be productive and forgive others. TYJ

February 17

You must get rid of the lies you tell yourself and replace them with facts. Saying you are sorry is not enough. Changing your behavior in your daily routine will help with the mistakes you have made in the past. That does not make you a bad person. You may have made bad choices based on faulty information. That does not mean you have to keep making them. When you feel alone and helpless, turn to God for your strength. Most of all, never give up and stop trying to be better than everyone else. Your aim is to be better than you were in the past. Fight depression with gratitude and living in today. Life may knock you down, but a grateful mind will find a reason to get back up. Do not let your past control you. Start by acting yourself into right thinking for God will fill your days with peace and serenity. You will be of use to mankind, your health will improve, and your nights will be restful. You will turn into that kind, loving, respectable person that God requires you to be. TYJ

February 18

God did not make you to be evil or foolish. He does not make junk. You made choices that caused you to be an addict, self-centered victim, co-dependent or a thief. For today, make a choice to fill that big empty hole in your soul with God's love and guidance. Do not get lost in hate or fear by making the choice to be kind and loving. Avoid fights. Do not let others control you. There will be good days and bad days. Be grateful for both, enjoy the good, learn your lessons from the bad. People or material possessions will not bring you the happiness you are so desperately seeking. That inner power to make good decisions starts with morning prayer and meditation. Your strength comes from within. You must let others be who they are meant to be for they must travel the journey they need to partake in to learn their lessons. Through it all, make the choice to stay positive, give unconditional love and show kindness. Pray for others to receive God's blessings and the ability to learn to choose wisely so their life can be filled with optimism and happiness. Do not let anyone destroy your inner peace. It is okay to let them be wrong. You are here to love and heal, not to be filled with rage and resentments. TYJ

February 19

Stay on your path of becoming a better person. With morning prayer and meditation and an evening inventory of self-examination, you will become the best version of you possible. Saying you are sorry for misdeeds of yesterday is great, not repeating them today is even better. You are starting today with a blank page, so make it a masterpiece. Being able to tell us from memory how an atom splits is nice. What is more important is having a loving heart, a listening ear and helping others; so, put your energy there. Cherish the people who love you for who you are. Most like you for what you can do for them, do it anyway and pray for the ones who could care less what you do. Family is not always kin folk. Hang with the people who put a smile on your face. Don't force anything today, just let things happen on their own. To make a difference in someone's life, all you must do is show them you care. With gratitude in your heart, you need to see the good in all situations. When you look in the mirror tonight, I want you to be able to say you did a really good job today. TYJ

February 20

Mental abuse is just as harmful as physical because it leaves emotional scars from controlling, disrespectful hurting words. Part of your spiritual growth is forgiving them, knowing they are sick people and may not realize how abusive they are. Ask what your lesson through all of this was for situations will not go away until you have learned from it. Through morning prayer and meditation, your answers will come. Start by looking at your part. Did you do anything to hurt them or are you insensitive to their needs? Set up boundaries by not allowing them to keep up their abusive behavior. You may not be able to walk away from the situation but that does not mean you have to put up with it. You do know that if the person has a narcissistic personality, none of this will work. Choose to spend the rest of your time here on Earth in peace and serenity. There will be times when you must get out of your comfort zone and walk in faith for God will put Light in your Darkness and love in your soul. TYJ

February 21

The Darkside wants you to fret about the future and to look back at your past with shame. Do not start your day with the broken pieces of yesterday. Some days are going to be better than others. With morning prayer and meditation, you can begin by looking for the good in each day and using positive thoughts to create your masterpiece. With God's guidance, you can handle anything the world throws at you. God's plan for you is better than anything you can work out so let go of what you thought your life should be like. You have made bad choices in the past. You don't have to let them control the rest of your life. You will find true peace by being grateful for the little aversions in your life by making everything an exciting event. TYJ

February 22

Hold on to the opportunity to change your thinking. Stop the loud chatty monkey voices that fill your mind with worry and anxiety. No matter how fractured you may have been, always hold onto the courage to be kind and loving to others. At a time in your life when you were defeated, confused and filled with grief, you wondered if you would ever make a change for the better. You may have cried and been consumed with rage, but you never gave up. The Darkside continued attacking you because you kept turning to God. You have made unhealthy choices in your life but that does not mean you are a bad person. If you think it, you can un-think it. Through morning prayer and meditation, you can and will improve your life. You must believe that God can do for you what you could not do for yourself. God does not care how much stuff you own or how pretty you are. He only cares how loving and kind you are today. Make pleasant memories while walking through your storm. Believe in miracles, take your Angels with you and you will end your day with a positive, grateful and loving heart. TYJ

February 23

Bad choices do not mean you are a failure. Sometimes you do the best you can with the information you have. With morning prayer and meditation, God will help you with having kind thoughts towards others. Celebrate your strengths. Be pleased that you won your silent battles and that you forgave others so you can heal. Be thankful that your blessings are bigger than your shortcomings. Be grateful for the people who have listened without judging and loved you no matter what. Today you will stop rationalizing and justifying your behavior by making excuses and will make an honest effort to become a better person. Look for the best in every situation you are confronted with for you know God will be there for you today. You are the keeper of your own happiness and will choose not to get angry today. TYJ

February 24

Sorry works for mistakes you make. It does not work on trusts that are broken and lives you have shattered. You will need to spend the rest of your life repairing those damages one day at a time. The Darkside will not give up the battle for you easily. Start with hope that there will be a light at the end of your dark tunnel. Battles take time for He will keep sending you negative energy. Do not overreact. It will take a lot of positive toughness to pull yourself out of your mentally dark place. With morning prayer and meditation, you will learn that you do matter, you are lovable and valuable no matter how broken you feel you are. Stop complaining about how bad your life is and what you don't have. Be grateful God woke you up today. TYJ

February 25

Seek the stillness of the morning to create the quietness with your inner voice. Listen to that soft gentle voice to receive guidance for the day. Believe in the power of prayer by trusting God, knowing that everything is going to be okay. He may not give the required information today, but He will answer your questions in His time. Do not create problems that don't exist by over thinking. Learn to release beliefs that no longer serve you and recognize new opportunities as God presents them to you. Heal the pain of the past with forgiveness. Worrying about what others think of you will make you a slave to them. Know that lessons not learned will be brought back until you do. At night, thank your Universal Power for all the learned behaviors knowing that you did your best with every deterrent the Enemy presented you with. The first thing to know is the Darkside will only have you obsessing more stuff or planting non-productive thoughts. God will present you with happiness from within. TYJ

February 26

Just for today, think about how good you have it, not how bad things are. You are 10x more appealing when you are soft and gentle then when you carry around the anger that comes from your hatred of yourself for you cannot love anyone else more than you love yourself. When you are critical of others, look at their defects that bother you and then apply them to you. Learning to love oneself is the most important thing you can do for others. Do what is best for your soul. Rest when tired, seek people who make you laugh when lonely. Helping others to love themselves will help you to get out of your funk. Turn your fears and anxieties over to God. The secret is to leave them in God's hands for this will help to bring joy into your life. TYJ

February 27

Today I will take that one small step to becoming a better person. A couple of things I have learned is that sometimes I am wrong and occasionally it is my fault and have make choices that maybe weren't the best. With morning prayer and meditation, I will ask God to help me speak the right words without anger in my soul. I have decided not to be rude, arrogant or a bully and to love others. I prefer to be the reason people smile. I know that if I have negative thoughts, it is impossible to have a positive life. I will not take what others say or do personally therefore I am no longer a slave to being hurt. I trust myself to make responsible choices. I get my strength from God, and I know who is fake and who matters. TYJ

February 28

Pay close attention to what triggers your reactions and dislikes of others for that may be where your childhood pain is still buried in your subconscious. This may take outside help to clear up the wreckage of your past. Learn to breathe in peace and breathe out old pain and anxiety. Things will get better if you don't live with the illusion that you don't have to work at your own recovery. It starts with morning prayer and meditation and the desire to improve my personal attitude. Pray for old garbage to be removed so both parties can be reconciled. Ask God to enter your life and turn around any bad situations you are having. He will bless you and your family and rebuild what needs to be healed. It is helpful to understand what part you played in all of this. May you find mending peace, gratitude and deep abiding joy today. TYJ

March 1

Think of your mind as a garden. With morning prayer and meditation, you can train your mind to be God centered, reacting with love and kindness. This would be planting flowers in your garden. Living in fear and self-centeredness is living with the Darkside or growing weeds in your garden. This does not just happen; you make the choice. Listen to your soft inner voice and ignore other people's gardens. Work on your own by planting seeds of positive love and abundance. Stay away from seeds of negativity, fear, sickness and lack. Satan plants fear of the unknown which causes you to stay in misery because it feels comfortable for it is all you know. Quit following the rules of the past and get on the new path to recovery. Believe in your abilities. Don't wait for things to get better. Learn to be happy where you are at right now. Choose to heal, not hurt. Help others to feel special. Stay away from fear, anxiety, guilt and shame and your garden will be a masterpiece. TYJ

March 2

You don't need to travel to far places to find change or spiritual growth. All the joy, wisdom and healing can be found within you. You will know you have achieved spiritual healing when you respond differently to life situations. How many times do you need to hurt or fail before you surrender to a power greater than yourself? With morning prayer and meditation, you can learn to ease the pain and suffering by releasing a better quality of life. Do you find offense with others, or do you understand that the actions of others have nothing to do with you? Your choice. Your dissatisfaction with your life is on you. Only you and God can rescue you. Self-love will help to fix your pain. Learn to surrender your problems to prayer. TYJ

March 3

If you think you have reached your limits and will never get better, then you won't. Let go of yesterday and focus on a new presence. Learn from your mistakes, failure is not an option. Do not let the loud chatty monkey voice drown out the soft gentle voice. If you are in a funky mood, the best thing you can do is remain silent for you will have less amends to make for misspoken words. Change is hard, believe in your heart that it will be worth the pain. The unpleasant emotional experiences you suffered will help you to want to make the choice to get better. God will not take the hurt away, but He will give you the strength to endure. Affirm that you will no longer look back with fear, anger or guilt. Take on a new attitude that you want to change and not that you must. Learn to travel your own path to freedom. Everyone is dissimilar. You are special and beautiful but different. See everything that is holding you back as temporary. Let go of past misconducts for you were fighting just to survive. Forgive yourself for giving all your power to the Darkside. Know your new strength of mind is God. Thank Him tonight for everything He has enthroned you with. TYJ

March 4

Misguided judgments made in the past are an important part of your change which will help create who you are today. The 1st thing you must realize is that nothing good can come from an angry negative attitude. The most painful segment of your previous dark past will help you to be compassionate for others seeking improvement. Only you are responsible for your own happiness. With morning prayer and meditation, you can respond to your day without the broken pieces of your past. Start a new chapter in your life with a new clean page for this is the 1st day of the rest of your life. Your mistakes and hard times from your past will give you the wisdom and strengths needed to become the new you. With God in your life, you can move forward with love and compassion. Modifying your old behavior will take time. Be patient. The Darkside will present obstacles and heartaches to prevent you from finding peace and serenity. Never give up, keep fighting to refine yourself. Just for today, may you seek happiness, joy and good health. TYJ

March 5

Take time to work on yourself. Do not speak a negative word, stay in the positive. Thoughts are energy so choose to fight the battles that will make you a strong, beautiful person. Listen to that soft gentle voice that tells you to pray and to help another person today. You are not responsible for fixing everything in the world that is broken or to make everyone happy. God cares for you. Seek Him in your morning prayer and meditation. Material things are not designed to make you happy, only God can do that. Do not let the pain and suffering of the past make you hard or bitter. Loved ones hurt you, finances or sickness may have plagued your life. Be thankful for everyday of your life. If God removes someone or something from your life, His intention is to replace it with something better. God will always be there to guide you. Keep the faith for He is your strength when you are lonely, sad or broken. TYJ

March 6

I am more impressed with how you handle your imperfections then how perfect you are. Life is short so follow your passions, do things that matter. The Enemy loves your dark side. God loves all of you no matter what you may have done. Others may have humiliated you, forgive. Face your realities by letting go of your perception of what you thought was real. Never assume you know everything. Recognize your limits, stay away from expectations and fear of failure. Choose to change any negative thinking so you can get better results. By changing panic attacks into faith, know that prayer will overcome any unpleasant emotions. During morning prayer and meditation, ask God for guidance. Just for today, do something good for another person. If you tell anyone what you did then you know you must work on your EGO. Choose to remain calm during a difficult time in your life. TYJ

March 7

Friends listen without judging. They helped, understood and loved you without conditions. In the quiet stillness, you will be guided during morning prayer and meditation. You have learned with prayer that nothing is going to happen today that God and you cannot handle. Your day will get better for God will restore peace and love in your life. When tempted to lose patience, remember all the times God and others have been patient with you. God will give you the strength to make it through any storm in your life. You needed the sadness before you could learn what happiness is and disturbance to appreciate silence. That feeling of emptiness, the hole in your soul, to welcome God's presence. Do not waste time on the foolish behaviors of others. Never allow anyone to disrespect you. Learn to let others drown in their own drama for it is not your job to fix them. May the knowledge of where you want to be, inspire you to become a better person. Bring hope to a seemingly hopeless day for ordinary things can become extraordinary by having God in your life. TYJ

March 8

Good morning fellow friends. May you start your day with a loving smile in your heart and happiness in your soul. If someone doesn't like you or has a self-imposed resentment against you, see them as a sick person who needs your prayers and love. Their anger hurts them, not you, just as your anger hurts you and not the other person. The Lord's prayer doesn't say, forgive me my trespasses and I will try to forgive others. Pay close attention to those words, "As I forgive others." You can remove your pain and achieve happiness by forgiving others. One kind word can end all that pain and misery and save a friendship with that person you choose to hate. Most importantly, it will save your life spiritually. Treating others with kindness is one of the most underrated experiences of finding the new you. Let go of anyone who chooses to leave. The part they played in your life may be over. Wish them well. Be grateful for the experience. TYJ

March 9

Be thankful for the difficult people in your life for they show you what you do not want to be like. Shoot for informed, not opinionated. The results of an angry person have far more reaching consequences than the cause. The Darkside will attack you if you become willing to seek God. He will plant a seed of fear of the unknown causing you to remain in misery. It is safe there for you know how you are going to react. The calm soft gentle voice of morning prayer and meditation is saying, "I want you to get excited about life again". I will help you with your challenges. The people I have sent to help you are already in place. Let go of that anger and trust in God. Learn to stay positive in one negative situation today so when the big one hits you; you will know what to do to handle it with ease. God only wants what is best for you. Being asked to forgive someone does not mean you have to send them an Easter basket. For your own freedom, peace and serenity you just must let it go. Your mind needs to be told to be grateful for your past and to accept it. Choose to do better today for the worst your past difficulties the bigger your rainbow. TYJ

March 10

Only your Higher Power can judge you. If you are prone to judging another, you lower your love and acceptance of them. You give a false evaluation of yourself which in turn sets into motion a devaluing of others. For today, learn to live by choice. Choose to listen to your Inner Voice and accept people with unconditional love. Be motivated to make changes in your life, starting with love of self, you will fill that empty hole in your soul so you can learn to accept others. Do not let anyone control your emotions. Changing your reaction to a situation has the power to change the circumstances. By not reacting with a negative attitude, you will find a positive solution. Be the good that happens to others. You will never regret it. Let go of what is hurting your soul. God has a purpose for your pain. Things will fall into place. You will receive the love and goodness you so richly deserve. TYJ

March 11

Decide what you want out of your new life. You will change, either because your mind has been opened or you have suffered enough pain. If God closed doors, it is because it is time to move on. Be thankful for the highs and the lows, for your joys and sorrows. Most of your pain comes from the way you respond to situations, not the way they really are. Don't shortchange old negative thinking. Trust the process, starting with morning prayer and meditation by being grateful for everything. Choose to offer love even if you feel hurt, angry or depressed. The new you needs to judge less and love more. The Darkside loves to reduce to rubble what is beautiful whereas God takes what is irreparably damaged and makes it absolutely wonderful. TYJ

March 12

Make the choice to let go of the need to be an extraneous factory trying to affect results. When judging, you feel in control. All you really get is unneeded stress and anxiety. Write down the situation that you want to command and give it to God. Transcribe it and put it in your God box to help make it real. Do not pretend everything is fine. By working on your reaction to what is happening around, you will need to pay attention to what you do when you don't get your way or how spiritual you are when someone criticizes you. Learning to let go of life situations is the quickest path to Inner peace. The old ways you learned to survive may not be the path you want to follow today. God is not finished with you yet. You are always capable of growing and healing more than you think you can. If your 1st opinion produced by your thinking is to look at everything with the refusal to see good thoughts, you will bring unfavorable results to all your life situations. Keep a positive attitude for God is bigger than anything you have going on in your life today. TYJ

March 13

If you don't believe in change, see how fast you can go from peace and serenity to fear, anxiety, panic and anger. Turn the page of that old life. Learn how to master calm and you will enjoy life. In the words or Waldo Emerson, "What you are doing shouts so loudly that I cannot hear a word you are saying." With morning prayer and meditation, learn to overcome your difficulties. Stop the madness for complaining causes you to become a victim. Either accept the facts or make the choice to change them by making peace with your past situations and people. Just for today accept yourself, be brave, and know that you are smart and loved. Never lower your level of quality to accommodate someone else. Be grateful for your friends who really care and will always take the time to listen. Evil will try to silence Good. TYJ

March 14

Feel your emotions, learn from them. Do not dwell on the adverse ones, allowing them to take up space in your thoughts which in turn helps them to become real. Do not stress about defeatist feedback from others. Pessimistic people project negativity. With morning prayer and meditation, everything will work out. Trust God and his wisdom. Make the choice to love yourself so you can love others. Stop blaming your parents, your job or your age. You made the choice. Just for today, choose to make better ones. Find a spiritual advisor you can trust with your innermost thoughts. You are given a free will so use it wisely to have faith rather than fear and to stay calm in every negative situation. You may not understand why right now but learn to trust the process. Admit your mistakes and move on. Only your EGO will keep you from swallowing your pride. No one is perfect. We fail. We forgive. We grow and learn, always working on becoming the person God desires you to be, not who someone else thinks you should become. TYJ

March 15

Do you blame, judge or criticize people? You are one decision away from a different life. Choose to examine your behavior. You are enough. Don't blame yourself for past failures for you cannot be everything to everyone. No matter your difficulties, choose to be kind and loving. With morning prayer and meditation, you can fill your life with blessings for it is how you handle yourself, not what has happened to you. Only you oversee your happiness so make wise choices that you can be grateful for later. Which voice are you listening to? The Darkside uses others to con you into making poor decisions and wanting more stuff. Be patient, focus on positive outcomes. Do good for others for everything comes back to you. Thank God for the blessings you do have. Stop stressing, trust God's plan for He knows what is best for your future. Spiritual growth is essential to your inner peace and serenity for it is not out there, it is within. TYJ

March 16

When trying to control others, you will end up frustrated and exhausted. Only you are responsible for your emotional attitude, not how they react to you. If you do not like how they react, change your ways. Keep your mind open to the circumstances of the good fortune for growth. If you want peace and contentment, let others be. Do less judging and reacting. Get rid of resentments and fears. When doing morning prayer and meditation, make the choice to have less chaos and more inner peace. Focus your attention on being positive and listen to the soft gentle voice for your answers. Just for today, affirm that you are not going to worry about or control others for it distracts you from your goal of serenity. Overthinking causes problems that don't exist. Do not obsess about what you don't have, trust that everything you need will be provided for. There is always something to be grateful for. Place your attention on the good that is going on in your life. Ask God to bless the people in your life and stop being so judgmental and critical. TYJ

March 17

God gave you the power to slay your own fears, worries and anxieties. Make the choice to turn them over to Him. Worrying, real or imagined, is an acquired behavior. If you have established the art of excessive anxieties, you can master the knowledge to let go of your lack of pleasure and follow the path to Inner Peace. God will heal what needs to be mended, your part is to walk away, if possible, from anyone who puts you down or does not see your worth. Surround your failures with loving kindness, starting with morning prayer and meditation. Do not allow your emotions to get the best of you. Those feelings of helplessness can lead to depression because there is no Universal Deity in your essence. Know that misfortunes or failures in your life make you stronger and help you to retain humility. God will keep you trudging the road to a happy destiny. Let go of anger and resentments. Put a smile on your face by forgiving them. Only you, with God's help, can change your inner being. TYJ

March 18

When doing morning prayer and meditation, look at how much time you spend helping others. Ask yourself, is the reason I spend all my time helping others is, so I don't have to look at myself? Do a list of things you want to be, beginning with patient, loving, happy and an awareness that causes you to feel worthwhile. You do realize if you want positive things to occur in your life, you are going to have to get off the couch and make them happen. React with staying away from negative people. Get excited about life. Do one thing each day that calls into question your old beliefs. Know that God has your back and will move you from anger and resentment to a peaceful, forgiving, loving person. Challenge God to send you a blessing today that helps you to get your life moving towards peace and serenity. No amount of shame will change your past and no feelings of anxiety will alter your future. Your energy will continue no matter who likes or dislikes you. Breathe in God's love, exhale all negative thoughts. God will replace the years the Darkside has stolen from you, with abundant resources and by bringing joy back into your life. TYJ

March 19

Life is too short to spend your time examining yourself as a failure. Reflect on your past as lessons learned. Envy of others may cause you to worry, complain, gossip and to compare your insides with others outside. Find one optimistic friend or Spiritual Advisor who is good for your mental health and will stick with you through all the phases of your life. Morning prayer and meditation is an excellent time to choose to make choices in your life. Focus on what is important. Be grateful. Believe that you are blessed, and that God loves you no matter what you may have done. You are responsible for your own happiness. Do not look outside of yourself for all your good comes from within. This morning, give God all your hurts, your worries, your doubt, your fears, your pain and your anxieties. Ask Him to put you on the path to recovery. You can bet if you do this the Enemy is going to come after you hard today. He wants you to be miserable. Whenever any of your old fears or anxieties start to come back, hit the pause button, ask God to remove any unwanted feelings. Tonight, don't forget to thank God for any blessings He has restored. TYJ

March 20

Start your day with morning prayer and meditation asking God to remove your biggest enemy. Fear. Choose to live in the moment. Worrying won't change a thing. It causes unhappiness for anxiety is disturbing to your soul. God will put your mind at ease when you seek Him by repairing your shattered life. Do not fear change, challenge your Demons. Open your mind to becoming a better person. Let people know when you are pleased with their actions. Acknowledge how great it is to be around them. Give them your best gift, your time. Get off your couch, put in the work necessary to become a better person. God knows your pains and will heal what is required to be restored. Learn to communicate your needs to others. Let your past propel you to become the person God wants you to be by spoiling whatever the Darkside had in mind. TYJ

March 21

Prioritize your list of things to do today. Give yourself a break. You do not have to do them all perfectly. Do the best you can today. You will make it and keep your sanity. Mistakes will be made. Your part is to learn from them. Just for today, make yourself a priority. Take some quiet time to figure yourself out. If someone is meant to be in your life, they will give you the time to heal. Teach people how to treat you right. Take time to learn how to communicate and be kind to others. Learn to listen for that is the greatest gift you can give them. Follow God's plan for you. It may be painful. Keep the faith, it will be worth it for He has your best interest at heart. TYJ

March 22

Take responsibility for your own actions. Blaming others sets you up to be a victim and is a characteristic component of a narcissist. Heal your emotions by choosing to remove anger, anxiety, selfish behavior and shame. Start by forgiving others and admitting one thing each day that you have done wrong. Study your habits so you can perceive reality and identify the truth. Continue to grow in love by respecting others. Know that they have their battles also. Gain the knowledge needed to cherish your memories with others. Just for today, thank all your amazing friends and family for being in your life. Be the best you can be for it is important what is inside your heart. Who you are is not really as important as what you are, so you can choose to be kind and loving. Thank God for waking you up today. TYJ

March 23

A perceived notion that your happiness will come from your new job, new house, new partner or a different wife or husband is part of your lack of self-love. With morning prayer and meditation, you will find true happiness comes from within. Learn to let God conduct your problems for He will heal your soul of any pain you have suffered. Let God negotiate your anxiety caused by fear and worries. You have made mistakes in the past. That does not make you a bad person, it only means you are human. You know how great God is because you have experienced his mercy. Focus on what you must gain. God hears your petition for help and will deliver what is most advantageous for you. Sometimes His desirable gift is an unanswered desire. TYJ

March 24

If you base your beliefs that others are your problem or you place the power of your happiness on someone or something that you have no control over, you condemn yourself to feelings of helplessness, hurt and resentments. You then become a victim. People will never love you enough or the way you want them to. If this is the path you choose, only you can fix your problems. No one can do it for you. Make the choice to change your beliefs with morning prayer and meditation. Just for today, make the choice to let God manage your emotions and heal your soul. Make your inner peace the most important project you will work on to becoming a better person. Learn self-love and you will never have to lean on another person or thing again. Know that if you do this, the Darkside will come at you with all His negative powers. Turn your day over to God and you will have the strength to conquer anything that the Enemy throws at you. TYJ

March 25

Just for today, show others that you care by making a difference in their lives. Only Light can force out Darkness. Our defects show up as a vile lack of love for self and others. With morning prayer and meditation, you can stop the game of "if only things had been different." Life is full of happy or sad times. Choose to walk away from people who disrespect your values or threaten your inner peace. Practice making better choices and increase your happy times. Fill your mind with positive thoughts. Increase your self-worth by respecting yourself. Start today with a blank page in your book of life. Do not let anyone write it for you. You can handle any situation that may challenge you today. Remember all the times you said you had feelings of regret? Now is the time to take the action to do something about them for sorry without action is procrastination. Your attitude will make a difference. Cruel words hurt others. Love will drive out hate. Choose God over Evil. TYJ

March 26

A healthy mental attitude starts by accepting yourself as you are today. With morning prayer and meditation, you will find your self-worth. The pain from feeling worthless will stop. You will learn to have patience and trust God's timing and know your Spiritual development is in God's hands. Just for today, complete unfinished tasks with enthusiasm. When making amends, know that it starts with what was your part and what can you do to make it right. With God's assistance, make this a day of accomplishments. Stay calm by letting go of what you can't control and practice kindness. Do not let your past define you. Instead, view it as lessons learned and let them strengthen you. Have a great day, stay positive and know something wonderful is about to happen. TYJ

March 27

You can either be critical of others or you can ask God to bless them. When judging others, you are saying they must act the way you want them to, or you will not love them. With morning prayer and meditation, you can choose to let go of the need to control others. Accept an attitude of living your own life and let others live theirs. When asking God to give you patience, it may not be granted. A calm mind is learned by acting not to react negatively. Happiness is the byproduct of doing what is right. Work on your own shortcomings, make amends by forgiving others and pay the money back. God does not spare you pain. He allows it to help draw you closer to Him. Through all this He will always be there for you. He will never give you more than you can handle, with His help. This isn't rocket science. Ask God for His assistance in staying calm, practicing self-control and right thinking. TYJ

March 28

Instead of talking about someone, try talking to them. Anger and resentments cause more harm to you than the person you are annoyed with. Be authentic for your actions tell others who you really are. True happiness comes from helping others, not from getting everything you want. Being at peace does not mean you will not have problems. What it really means is you have quieted that loud chattering monkey voice in your mind. You have stopped overthinking and have faith that God will work everything out. You can learn something from everyone if you take the time to watch and listen. Look for the good in others and good will find you. Know that whatever irritates you about them, just maybe your worst defect. Practice letting things go. Breathe God in, exhale worry. Stay calm, God is watching over you today because anxiety will not fix a thing. TYJ

March 29

What is your purpose in life? What is gnawing away at your gut? What is your Soul trying to get you to do? Learn to listen to that soft gentle voice during morning prayer and meditation. If you have cleared away all anger and resentments, you will easily be able to hear that voice. Find out what you were born to do. What are your passions in life? It is never too late to start on your reason for being. Look at the lies the Enemy has been telling you that have been holding you hostage. He wants you to believe there is no God. Just for today, when surrounded by drama and gossip, don't join in. this is the 1st day of your new life. So, take a minute to think about how well you have it. Appreciate life as you have come to live it. Know that self-control is a strength and that you have mastered calmness by not letting the insignificant actions of others steal your joy. Show love and kindness to all for God only cares how you treat them. TYJ

March 30

Never regret the past. You spend a lot of time judging yourself. Start with forgiving and accepting. Learn to look at yourself with a positive attitude, seeing a kind loving person. With constructive affirmations, you will become that person. Go make a difference in someone's day by inspiring a soul to enjoy their day. You do not need anyone's approval to start your life over. When doing morning prayer and meditation, picture yourself filling with the light of the Universe. You will be safe, bubbling with confidence as you start to fulfill your purpose in life. You need to quiet that loud chatty monkey voice in your mind so your Spiritual or Emotional intellectual Energy can apply knowledge, sound reasoning and constructive thinking. Do not question the little things God asks you to do. TYJ

March 31

One of the many choices I make each morning is whether I will spend my day in faith or worry. Do I take on a critical judgment demeanor or do I look at my own shortcomings with a humble attitude? Am I grateful for my friends who are not considered my family? Have I learned to stay clear of negative people who have a new catastrophe for every solution? Do I take a fear that has consumed me, done research while looking at the possibilities of it happening? With morning prayer and meditation, do I ask God to remove my anxieties knowing in my immortal being, that God has everything covered? If by chance all I get done today is to be a better person than I was yesterday, then today will not be a total loss. Through it all, I have put forth the effort to love myself while challenging me personally to keep enhancing my Spiritual being. I also need to work on improving my health for we all have 2 parts to use. An immortal deity and a body. TYJ

April 1

With morning prayer and meditation, you will attain an imperturbable peace at the root of your spirituality. Your intuition has you showing emotional sensitivity, reacting positively with a newfound awareness of being alive. You have come to grips, learning to live with your past, realizing that everything that happened helped to make you the strong person you are today. You feel void of any conflict and turmoil, having gained the knowledge that your happiness must start with you. You choose to start your morning working on the prospect of becoming a better person. You have perceived the confidence to sit in quiet meditation, to discover God's purpose for your life. You find the courage to be yourself and do not have to compare yourself to others. Begin today with one positive thought, by making the choice, to train your mind to see enjoyment in your life. TYJ

April 2

With morning prayer and meditation, you can generate a way out of your problems. Miracles do happen, never stop believing because God rewards those who earnestly seek Him. Situations happen to cause change, so keep a watchful eye on what is occurring around you. See the best in people but focus on their actions for circumstances and conditions can change quickly. Find your purpose in life and follow God's plan. You no longer must live in fear. Set your goals for the pursuit of happiness and living a wholesome life. Tell others you love them. Make your story the best in the world for your past was not a life sentence. Its purpose was to help you to seek God along with making you a compassionate, gentle, deep loving person. Your lessons have taught you to be strong but gentle, fierce but understanding, along with gaining the knowledge that peace is more precious than perfection. You are responsible for your own happiness so choosing to become a better person will help to implement those feelings. TYJ

April 3

Real change starts with your thinking. If you have a quarrelsome disposition, you will have strife in your life. Have an awareness of circumstances going on around you if for no other reason then why certain situations happen in your life. A bad choice usually ends up with a crappy outcome so take the time to gain the knowledge to take care of yourself by replicating a novel behavior educated by others because lessons gained from your mistakes will get you on the path to making better ones. When possible, walk away from people who cause you strife by letting your newfound Spirituality shine through and likeminded people will be attracted to you. Be grateful for what you have found out about yourself. Inner peace of mind comes from a positive attitude. Choose to start your day with God's love by participating in morning prayer and meditation. Be sure that what you are praying for is what you really want. Good health comes from a lack of stress and anxiety. Fill your day with love, laughter and tranquility. Take the time to slow down, rest and reflect on your goals for a happy life. God is telling you that material things are nice although not the most important. TYJ

April 4

By evaluating my expectations of my behavior, I look at my reaction to others. Do I expect to be liked and approved by everyone? With continued work on myself, I have come to the realization that I can only please God and myself. I will live my life and be happy. With morning prayer and meditation, I will swallow my pride and admit when I am wrong. How others feel about me is none of my concerns. How I react when someone disapproves or criticizes me is a function of mine. I no longer think God must meet all my desires. Today I have chosen to grow up and follow God's plan for my purpose in life. I am responsible for the effort. God is responsible for the outcome. I have concluded that all I can do is accept life on life's terms and be the best version of me possible, being aware that I am better than no one. I choose to react with love and kindness. I have gained the knowledge that may not be the other person's goal. I pray that God gives you the strength to conquer all your adversities and may He bring hope to your spiritual life. TYJ

April 5

Never allow anyone to make you feel less than human. You will be presented with areas to work on so deal with any challenges that come into your life today. Do not procrastinate or put off until tomorrow. The 1st thing you must do is to relax through morning prayer and meditation. Anxiety can cause destructive, negative and irrational thinking and prevents the normal action of the mind. You need to be in a receptive and responsive state of mind in order to constructively work through your problems thus becoming a better, stronger person. Under no circumstances do you go back to your old, failed way of thinking. You will find your purpose in life by listening to the soft gentle voice that will reveal any action you need to take with coincidences and intuition. You make the choice to be blessed or stressed so learn to control your reactions. Pause, observe and proceed with restraint of tongue for God will give you the strength to carry out any action He wants you to set into motion, allowing you to achieve your goals. Learn to meet your problems with joy and overcome them. View your hardships as an opportunity for growth. It is important to learn from the bad choices and mistakes you have made in the past by allowing a Higher Power, a Spirit of the Universe, to enter your life. TYJ

April 6

Take this opportunity to devote time with yourself. Do you love yourself enough to be able to utilize time alone? Your negative thinking will limit God. The Darkside wants to restrict your growth. Do not be chained to your old way of thinking. God can turn around every bad situation in your life. He will heal old wounds. You are not held accountable for what happened to you as a child. Your parents or guardians did the best they could with what they had. You do have an obligation for today. Do not wallow in the past. Your part is to open your intellect to love and kindness and allow positive thinking to enter your psyche. Do not look without for the things you need are from within. Take this time of being to slow down and find out what is important in your life. Food, water, transportation and basic shelter are outside requirements. Anything else is looking beyond your inner necessities. You are the master of your fate and God has entrusted you with independent decision making. The Enemy will cause fear, panic and anxiety and can only tempt you with outside stuff. With morning prayer and meditation, you will receive the power to fight these negative thoughts. You create your own world by your reflections and possibilities. Why not start today with positive scrutiny and better reasoning? TYJ

April 7

Your most precious gift you have to offer is love and kindness which does not cost you anything. Why some choose to contribute nothing, but fear and anger is beyond me. Being controlled by the Darkside, they harm themselves and contribute nothing to the Universe. By being strong in your faith, you do not accept their behavior and they in turn will have a bad day. Those of you who have trained your mind to stay calm and positive do not allow others to ruin your day. You do not chase after people to be your friend. You work hard on your positive attitude and attract the right people to join you in your journey. You have learned the art of forgiveness. By learning to love yourself, 1st you put your trust in God, knowing He will turn around every bad situation presented to you today. With morning prayer and meditation, you can decide on a course of action to become a better person along with having a great day when your thinking, saying and doing are all in harmony. That becomes who you are, glorifying the Universe with your aggregate qualities and senses of pleasurable abilities, exalting a triumphant joy in the Spiritual development of others. TYJ

April 8

Is your life a statement of love and kindness for yourself and others? When you talk about people, places and things you love, do you mention yourself? If your answer is no to these, you have a starting point to work on for your morning prayer and meditation. If your answer is yes, we need to hear how you got there. How you struggled and what your journey was like. How the magic happened. How you went from a fearful, irritable and distorted imagination because of negative circumstances and neurotic thinking to a calm peace-loving person who has found God. How you went from, "I can't" to "I can do all things". From, "I felt all alone" to being filled with love and compassion for your fellow human beings. All your worries disappeared and how you feel blessed. How you have been freed of the negative burdens of life and giving a life of freedom and harmony. We are all on a journey. Your choice today is, is it going to be joyous or is it going to be filled with anger and resentments? You are the only one standing in your way to becoming happy, joyous and free. Believe in yourself, trust the process and know that some storms are meant to clear your path. Pause, be silent and realize how blessed you are. If life is tough today, just do the next thing the Universe puts in front of you. TYJ

April 9

Your Ego has you thinking you are always right, and it causes you to see the world through rose-colored glasses. It gives rise to your living in fear and fantasy thinking that life is one big problem. It is your inner critic giving rise to your playing the part of the victim. Everyone is out to get you. You suffer from recessive anger because your past reactions have caused you negative backlash at work and home, so you stuff your strong feelings of displeasure which in turn triggers inner turmoil. You blame others for your irritability, distorted imagination and erotic behavior. You find fault with everything and allow false values to control your conduct. Once you find out how to accept Life on life's terms, all this becomes mere incidents. You master the art of turning your will and your thinking over to God. Through morning prayer and meditation, you receive a realistic view of life and react to situations with calmness. You acquire the knowledge to cope with problems instead of having them control you. God has become your refuge and your fortress. Be the reason someone reacts with love and kindness today. What the Darkside sent to destroy you has made you the strong sensitive understanding person you are today by expressing the Universal method of human communication by showing an intense feeling of deep affection. TYJ

April 10

If you fail to temptation, it is never God's fault. Which voice are you listening to? You need to know and understand the Enemy. He is cunningly powerful at putting thoughts into your mind that appear to be very logical. The Darkside will continue to poison your mind by telling you that you deserve more of the best stuff. It isn't really stealing, you earned it. True happiness is making the choice to be satisfied with what you have for God will ensure you have everything you need. Except your life for what it really is, not what you think it should be. Use positive thoughts. Eliminate "cannot, try and never" from your vocabulary. You are enough. You are a whole, complete person by yourself. Stay in the moment. Observe rather than react. Anger will affect you physically and emotionally. Practice relaxing exercises by turning your tensions over to God and not allowing anxiety to enter your mind. If you have been suffering the same pains over and over, it is because you have not taken the time to learn your lessons. With morning prayer and meditation, accept God's love and you will light up the world. Be the delightful person God has deemed you to be. Have true faith that everything will turn out for the best. TYJ

April 11

Being an observer gets you out of self. You have gained the knowledge to not follow your misguided ideas and have made room for God's blessing by letting Him handle your problems. He will heal your hurts and put an end to your worries. You stop choosing negativity, anger and revenge and instead wisely choose optimism, compassion and forgiveness. You find when previous situations have lost their hold on you or stopped causing you pain. You have learned your lessons. When you give, you receive happiness for takers are never satisfied and always want more. You base your action on values instead of personal gain. In the past, you may have reacted with negative outbursts. You know that God can handle the outcome without your help. You no longer play games and mean what you say and do not expect others to read your mind or feel the need to force others to like you. What circulates is God saying yes and what does not work out is God saying no. you have stopped dictating outcomes and have immersed yourself in the enjoyment of the process of live and let go. Do not let the jerks of the world ruin your day. TYJ

April 12

Be willing to admit your part in any situation and seek forgiveness. Do not let your ego stand in the way. If you wait for karma to make you humble, it won't be pretty. No matter how dark it gets, what is broken or hurt can be fixed. Just remember, as bad as you may want to, you cannot fix others. You can talk about morning prayer and meditation and how it has affected your life. You can teach concern, tenderness, understanding, deliberation and consideration. You cannot force anyone else to accept God in their life. They must do that on their own. You can only love and pray for them. There is only one of you and that is the part God has chosen you to play. Be who your soul says you are, not what you think others want you to be. Let God's light shine through you for it is impossible to change if all you see is darkness. Just for today, ask God to contain your anger so as not to cause anyone to have a bad day. Instead, inspire one person to have a better day. There's a spiritual axiom that says if at any time I have a thought of anger, I, not them, am at fault. Slow your mind down and if you so desire choose to walk with God. TYJ

April 13

What is your goal for today? Are you going to start with, "I want to become a better person" as your 1st achievement? Are you going to look at yesterday to see who you hurt and owe an apology to? What action do you need to do today so as not to make the same bad choices and mistakes? What was your Darkside selling that you bought into? Are you going to continue to blame others for your behavior, shortcomings and misfortunes? Hurt people, hurt others. It is your emotions and imperfections that make you who you are. You will make the choice to want to alter your defects for 2 reasons. You have learned sufficient possibilities to want to improve or your pain is abundantly severe causing you to want it to go away and the only way that will happen is to modify your behavior. When faced with 2 or more possibilities through morning prayer and meditation, will you listen to your Higher Power and take responsibility for your actions while looking at your behavior and make attempts to perceive better communications today. Whose point of view will you listen to? TYJ

April 14

You are asked to show Mercy instead of lashing out when you feel the pain of being hurt. Do not let the fear of disappointment or rejection control you. Participate in your own recovery through morning prayer and meditation, working on stabilizing your mind so as not to react to your conscious physiological behavioral change by not responding to negative people. Part of mastering self-control over your state of feelings is how you respond to situations around you. Learn to judge less and accept what is happening as part of God's plan. Think positive intentions because you spend a lot of time with mental activities so make it a nice place to visit. You have to unlearn cultural conditioning which causes inaccurate conclusions. Other people's opinions are not who you are. When confronted with times of uncertainty; stop, take a deep breath and ask God to help you through this. At first this will feel uncomfortable. Let God fill that big empty hole in your soul which may be caused by loneliness, the pain of a loss or a lack of a Power greater than yourself. Your Darkside will want you to fill that hole with drugs, people or stuff for that is all He has to offer. Instead, seek God's guidance to find your purpose in life starting with, "He does want you to help others by giving of yourself." TYJ

April 15

Today can be the beginning of a bright new life. Be grateful for what you have and embrace the teachings. If you are new to this purpose thing, know that God wants you to start with helping others. He will give you more to handle as you improve your life. It can be nothing more than a compliment. I am saying to you that you are enough and a delight to be around and since God made only one person like you, you are irreplaceable. If you are going through hard times right now, embrace the lessons for they are meant to lead you to your objectives in life. The harder your times, the bigger your achievements will be. Forgive those who have deeply offended you Do something new today that God has been challenging you today to do by starting your morning with prayer and meditation. Make an honest effort to spend some quiet time with God focusing on your goals in life. He never intended for you to sit around and feel sorry for yourself. When observing others take notice of those who appear to be the most content, happy people for they are the ones improving themselves. The unhappy ones, taking inventory of everyone else and trying to improve them. TYJ

April 16

More does not mean better. Take time during the day to be grateful for all God has given you. Through morning prayer and meditation, create a positive lifestyle by making the decision to become a desirable person. Do one thing today to make someone's life better. Take the time to find the most favorable in others and you will discover the finest in you. Make a special effort to have God in your life today. Happiness begins with you, not who you know or what you own. If being in the limelight brought on true happiness and showing of love, then people in Hollywood should be the most joyful of human beings in the world. With God's love, you can make true friends and receive opportunities for growth. Create a mindset of peace and serenity. Do not allow anyone's bad behavior to ruin your day. Having a job doesn't always mean more stuff. You could choose to do good for others. Create a world of affection and tenderness filled with laughter and peace by making the choice to welcome the act of caring for others into your life. Above all, learn to forgive those who have hurt you. TYJ

April 17

God dislikes false pride. Stop thinking you are better than your actions. Take a thoughtful daily inventory of your defects. If you treat others with negativity, you are a negative human being. Own it. Make the choice to set it as a goal to become a better individual today. If you persist on doing what you always did, you will resume to be what you always were. A self-centered egotistical child. Bad choices made in the past are not meant to be a life sentence. Before you can receive optimism and growth you will need to tear down the barriers that the Darkside has built up in your being. You were never meant to live in a defeated, ashamed, depressed state of mind. What do you do about it? You do whatever it takes. Trying to get better is not doing. You either do it or you don't. With morning prayer and meditation, you ask God to help you to become a better intelligent being. You learn to walk the face of the Universe honestly with dignity and integrity. What is your choice, negative or positive? I pray you make the choice to improve. TYJ

April 18

Listen to the soft gentle voice of your spiritual side. Sometimes it whispers or pulls. Other times it pushes. Your immortal self will always take you where you need to go. On the other side of it, the loud chatty monkey voice must get you to believe a lie once you know the truth. It will be different this time. You deserve to be happy. Learn to play the tape all the way through. With morning prayer and meditation, God is ready to deal with your damaged soul. Have you cleared the way with forgiveness and the releasing of all your resentments? You may have had a meltdown for you are human after all. Have a good cry, let it out. Focus on today. You know you are growing when you feel awkward and uncomfortable. You display feelings of anxiety seeing someone or thing as dangerous, painful or threatening and unfamiliar. Ask God to remove your distressing emotion, whether it's real or imagine, for it causes feelings of dread and apprehension. God will be with you while you take the risk of becoming a better person. Choose not to go back to your old normal self by seeing it for what it really is. Self-destruction caused by the Darkside. TYJ

April 19

Be cautious of the loud chatty monkey voice in your head for it is not connected to the Universe. This is the voice that says this is the way you always did it and it is good enough. You do not need the change. Do not limit your future by staying in your past circumstances. You are not powerless over your life situations. With morning prayer and meditation, you will receive the power of selflove. If you can rise above the voice of the Darkside, you stand an excellent chance of survival. Love the people whose behavior towards you is the worst for it is important to love yourself no matter how others deal with you. Be independent and love yourself enough to make the choice to choose a better quality of friends. Take responsibility for your future growth by cleaning up your past without shame. Work on your dignity and respect by choosing to be the finest you can be. Do not let fear or anxiety direct your thinking. Forget the blunders and absurdities you made yesterday. Start today with the faith that everything will work out 1st rate if you take God along on your journey. TYJ

April 20

The difference in my life before and after I started morning prayer and meditation was that I always had to be right. I never cared about anyone's feelings. I was positive that my way was the only way. I reacted to every situation with the attitude of "what can you do for me?", so if I was nice to you, it was because I needed you to do something for me. I felt I was better than you but I needed you to like me so I could like myself. My life was filled with shame and regrets. I stuffed my rage to the point of causing me to suffer from depression. Everything I did was to gain attention. I would brag about how great I was and being truthful was not an option. I talked about others, pointing out their character defects. I told you whatever I thought you wanted to hear. After years of morning prayer and meditation, I now know that I am the problem and I believe I have found a solution. I have God in my life, and I work on being the opposite of the above-mentioned shortcomings. I start my day with an optimistic outlook on life while keeping my goals and purpose in mind. I believe that no matter what happens today, I will not react with the inability to see the truth. I replace every detrimental thought with 2 positive ones. Let go of the things you have no control over by breathing God in and contradictory views out. I am grateful that I no longer must play the role of being a victim. I view life with love and acceptance of myself and others. TYJ

April 21

On 4/21/16 I sent out my 1st morning meditation to 7 people. It read, "What are you going to do if you find yourself agitated?" Today I will send it out to 84 people in 11 states and Canada. I have no idea how many people this message is shared with. I am humbled that God shares this message with me to pass on to you. On 4/21/21, what are you going to do if you find yourself agitated today? Angry people lash out to show you how powerful they are. Inner peace begins when you choose not to allow others to direct your behavior responses. Name the agitation and know how it impacts your serenity. When working on becoming a better person, know that you are worthy. Haven't you destroyed your inner peace and serenity enough? It starts with staying away from negative people when possible. God may have chosen you to bring that person out of the darkness. Life is too short to have regrets. Everything happens for a reason. Life may not have been easy, but it made you who you are today and today is all you are promised. Make it a masterpiece by making the choice to bring God into your life seeking his guidance and forgiveness, praying the damage you did was not too severe. May your day be filled with love and kindness and your emotions gentle and filled with hope. Participate in your own recovery by getting up off the couch and making the choice to learn from your past failures, moving forward wiser and full of gratitude. TYJ

April 22

May God establish peace in your world today. Know that serenity starts with recognizing the lies your Darkside is telling you that are holding you hostage. Stop living the life that others tell you to live while blaming them for your problems. With morning prayer and meditation, you can learn to define yourself as lovable. You first must forgive your self-doubt and thank God for giving you your life back. Know that God will heal the source of your pain. With positive thoughts, you can change your behavior which in turn will improve your quality of life by helping you to recover from mental stress. Learn to take the good with the bad. Be grateful for what you have. Forgive all those who have deeply hurt you and learn from your past misfortunes. The world continues to move on. You make the choice to do either the positive or the negative rotation. TYJ

April 23

Be on the right side of Goodness in the Universe. With morning prayer and meditation, you will remain teachable, gentle, patient and humble while acquiring the knowledge of loving yourself and others. You can help another by listening, praying for them and giving advice when asked. You cannot stop the pain others are suffering because of the consequences of their bad choices, behavior and actions. You need to remind yourself, if you didn't cause it, you are not responsible. There will be no solution for them until they realize they alone are the problem and hold their own key to freedom. You may be the light needed for others to be brought out of the darkness. We are in each other's life for a reason. Know when to walk away from those who don't value you. When given a compliment, your response is, "Thank you". Reflect on the hardships you went through knowing your one true strength was that you never gave up. Your biggest misfortune was and always will be your resistance to change. One thing you did learn was that you always came out of the storm a better, stronger person. Where the pains of change worth it? Yes, every time. I must remember I am a Spiritual Being sent down to earth to learn the lessons needed to survive in the Universe and I will keep coming back until I learn them. TYJ

April 24

Be true. Be positive. Be calm always. Most stressful situations come from how I respond to perceived problems, real or imagined. Today I will adjust my attitude and trust the soft gentle voice from within. I will not let my emotions overpower my intellect or the insignificant action of others affect my mood. I will be the master of my calmness, showing strength that comes from starting my day with morning prayer and meditation. I will ask God to help me when I allow the behavior of others to ruin my day. I pray that I will receive the intuition that I, not them, am the problem. Only then will I find the solution to my frustrations. That pertains to everything going on in my life today. Part of mastering inner peace is not responding to toxic negative people. Be who God created you to be. Show compassion and kindness to others especially emotionally sick family members through the insight and ability to make sound judgment through the power of prayer. TYJ

April 25

May the love and kindness of God enter your heart today. Through morning prayer and meditation, let the soft gentle voice of God into your soul so you may make sound choices today. Start letting go of resentments for the wrongs of others have done to you. There are nasty people in the world who do harm to others. The loud chatty monkey voice will tell you the only way to handle them is with rage. The Universe has a system set up to handle this. It is called Karma. God will only fight your battles after you have forgiven the person. Therefore, it is so important that we stop blocking ourselves from the Sunlight of the Spirit. Do not believe the loud chatty monkey voice from the Darkside when he tells you this is not true. Let God bring light into your darkness by having faith that He will fight your struggles for you. We are not perfect. We all make wrong judgments based on faulty, inadequate knowledge. Be grateful for the people who look beyond our defects and make the choice to love us anyway. TYJ

April 26

Only God can judge the real you. Surround yourself with kind, loving people who see the good in you. Give yourself a break today. Worries take away today's peace. Put all your fears and anxieties into the hands of your Higher Power. He will gladly carry your burdens for you, protecting your loved ones, keeping them safe during these trying times. He will heal the brokenness in others. Your unhappiness is caused by your thoughts about any negative circumstances, not the actual situation. Your part is to see every situation for what it is. What was your part? Forget what they did, what did you do? The loud chatty monkey voice will con you into believing the problem is them. No. You are your worst enemy. Always do your best, leaving the outcome to God. Stop being so hard on yourself, change takes time. The 1st step is you wanting to improve your life. Starting with selflove and giving yourself the same loving care, you afford others, unless you are still a selfish self-centered egotistical person. Then you may want to learn to treat others better. TYJ

April 27

Don't be a victim. It's "I feel" not "you did". Dear God, help me to realize that my decisions are my responsibility, and I am not to blame others for the outcome. Focus on yourself, not what you think others should be doing. Do not change your beliefs just to satisfy the feelings of others. You will do it because you know it is right and you want to make the change. You will move forward when you let go of the shame for past transgressions and forgive yourself. You are responsible for your own happiness. With morning prayer and meditation, and the help of your Higher Power, you no longer feel powerless over your past. Thinking you have that power by yourself is an illusion. No matter how small the positive action you take, it will have an impact on your life. You do have the ability to change and become better. What is important is what you can teach others from your experience, not what your wealth will buy for them. Teach them to focus on the good and to never give up for you have no idea how close you are to success. May you have a day filled with God's blessings. You will always do your best and refrain from critical self-judgment. When tired, lonely or angry. Rest and pause for you will make lousy decisions otherwise. TYJ

April 28

Put love into action. Don't hate yourself for what you are not. Be grateful for who you are. Make a list of your strengths. Formulate your life around your best characteristics or traits. Be a shiny example for others to frame their life after. Seeking approval of others is not a natural characteristic. Make sure your life is flowing in harmony with your spiritual attributes so you can receive your intuitions and creative ideas. If you spend all your time talking to God, you leave no time for listening. Allow God to fill that empty hole in your soul with peace and serenity. The Universe will help you bring all this together to give you your purpose in life. May you find yours now. Take the time to let God talk to you through morning prayer and meditation. It is the most important thing you can do but it is the 1st thing you don't do. Take time to walk with nature. Your Darkside does not want you getting your directions from God. He will fight you all the way on this. You must learn to quiet that loud chatty monkey voice in your head, for until you do, your life will be filled with unhappiness, self-indulgence and fear. Learn to relax. Stop taking everything personally, for this is the root of your self-centeredness. Learn to live life calmly with your strength coming from God. TYJ

April 29

The bigger the storm, the better the rainbow. What have you learned from life's lessons? All the knowledge in the world is useless without a heart full of love and kindness while supporting a willingness to help others. Do not try to do everything by yourself. Through morning prayer and meditation, you learn to rely on a loving God to help you through all of life situations. If you only give God one avenue to get your attention, life will be full of pain and suffering if you do not seek the will of God. A negative mind will never get positive results. You are designed to expand your life through finding your purpose. Do not spend your time looking at avenues God has closed. Staying who you are while becoming a better person is part of God's strategy for you. Embrace God and you will receive the gifts of peace and serenity. Your choice: self-control or seek God's design for you which will get you connected to the Universe and started on your intention for being. TYJ

April 30

Are your expectations of yourself and others realistic? If others are continually disappointing you, you may need to lower your anticipations of them. Do you hold high moral standards for yourself? Is this the life you want to live, or can you do better? It is not being selfish to set boundaries. It is called taking care of yourself. Stop letting people use you. With morning prayer and meditation, you will receive the power to decide who you want to help and when. You do not have to rush out at 3am just because someone is having a problem. Don't forget to reserve some me time. Make plans to go on mini vacations or retreats. No is a complete sentence. Learn to say it without feeling guilty or having to explain why you had to say it. The best way to see God's hand in life situations is to make the choice to leave them in His hands. You will fail, make mistakes and get hurt for after all you are human. With God's assistance, you will rise, learn your assignment with gratitude, knowing the pain will diminish in time. Hurtful moments will enter the life of your loved ones. Let them know how much they mean to you; not how weak you perceive them to be. Show them a loving God who is willing to help. TYJ

May 1

Learning to be comfortable with your own company is a first step in learning to love yourself. Some days will be easier than others because bad choices made in the past will come back to haunt you. You must accept the fact that you are human, and humans are not perfect. Forget your past mistakes but hang on to the lessons. You are not in competition to be better than anyone else. With morning prayer and meditation, you can count on the fact that God will be there to help you through the tough times while helping you to clean up your feelings of superiority, egotism and negative attitude. Work on being better than you were yesterday. For some, that will never be satisfactory. Forget them, be acceptable for yourself. Each one of us has our own strengths and weaknesses. My strengths will help other's weaknesses and theirs mine. Discomfort comes in many forms. Some are physical, others are mental, still others emotional and lastly spiritual. Be aware of your suffering so you can get in touch with the Universe for help. I thank you in advance for any help you may be assisting me with today. TYJ

May 2

Do what makes you happy, just make sure you are following God's plan. He will increase your inner strengths and your power will know no limits. Life will always be complicated. Don't take on life's responsibilities on your own. Bring God into your daily routines. When others give you their opinion on how you should run your life, it is usually based in what is best for them. If you don't go after what you want, you will always be the same. Stop fretting over things you can't change. Don't feel like life is good or bad. Look at it as what is God teaching you today. Your choice is how do you react to it? What is your lesson? God lets the whole process up to you and whether you want to participate in your recovery. Through morning prayer and meditation, you learn to leave everything in God's hands. You develop a strong faith that He will help you with your daily burdens while relieving you of your fears. Be grateful while staying patient for the many blessings God will bestow upon you today. Hanging with positive people will bring you to places you never thought possible. Take time to thank Him for loving you and never leaving your side. TYJ

May 3

Accept yourself as the beautiful person you are. Be in love with God, yourself and your neighbor. With morning prayer and meditation, you can enjoy nonstop blessings and joy. Every person you meet is sent for a reason, some bad but mostly good. The negative, Darkside people will use and abuse you. The good are sent to save your life by helping you out of the darkness that Satan has you trapped in. Don't wait for the storm to pass. Learn to dance in the rain. The enemy tried to break you but failed. You are still here fighting for our life by not reacting to the toxic people around you. All the education and money in the world will not make you wise or generous. The kindest people usually have the biggest scars. Don't regret your past. Walk through today with confidence and face the future with God's grace and love. Thank God for the people he sent to bring out the best in you. God will never put you into situations that you can't handle, if you don't try to do it on your own. God is making a difference in your life by mending what needs to be healed. TYJ

May 4

Nothing goes away until it teaches you the lesson you needed to learn. You are given a free will to make your own choices on how you react to life situations. Remember it is not important what people say or do to you. What is far reaching, or paramount is how you react to them. Know your Enemy. Your Darkside wants you to react with hate and anger, causing you to have an ugly heart. Satan wins every time you choose to act with a critical assessment of others. Being in a hurry can have a profound effect on your success, survival or wellbeing causing you to be overwhelmed with anxiety and anxiousness. Don't be so busy denying your mistakes that you can't learn from them. God uses pain and suffering to get your attention. Through morning prayer and meditation, learn to let God help you fight your battles. He gives you more than you can handle on your own. He is begging you to seek His assistance in your daily routine. Stop living in the absence of your Spiritual life. Instead, seek your new beginnings. Keep fighting for your life. Someday it will all make sense. Keep doing your best for what is meant to be will always find its way. TYJ

May 5

When a toxic person can no longer control you, they will sway others to see you as a bad person. When setting your boundaries, do not worry about the abusive person's feelings. You need to learn to take care of yourself. It will feel strange at first to choose to make better choices. Your objection to change can be painful. The destructive person will always reflect everything back on you. It is your fault that they are unhappy. They possess the ability to bring you down to their level, confusing you with their BS and leaving you feelings emotionally exhausted. Rarely will you bring them up to your level. With morning prayer and meditation, you will receive the gift of humility. You learn that you are different from others but not better than anyone else. Spirituality will teach you that you must love and forgive the emotionally unhealthy person. You can choose to but do not have to continue to accept them into your life. You will acquire the skills needed to survive without feeling guilty. Give up the notion that this time will be different with the negative person just because you have changed. TYJ

May 6

Let go of anger and resentments for they will kill your soul. Don't allow people to see you at your worst. If you are critical of everything and everybody along with too high of expectations, you are going to be unhappy. Why do you choose to live that way? Do you want people to remember you by what you said you were going to do or by what you have accomplished in life because you took the action to change? Making the choice to change starts with your daily routine. Through morning prayer and meditation, God will remove your bitterness, sorrow, depression, anxiety and fears. You will never again have to live with an ugly soul. Fight to become a better person. Your opposition to change will be your biggest obstacle to change because the Darkside wants you miserable. Why would you choose to remain a mess when life can be such a joyful experience? Concede to your innermost self that God is good. When your time on Earth has ended, God is not going to judge you on how big your bank account was but rather on how big your heart was and what you did to help others. TYJ

May 7

Your spiritual journey is told by feelings, not dates. Just for today, row your own boat instead of causing chaos by rocking everyone else's boat. Your own happiness can only come from you. Have the faith, courage and wisdom to give your anxieties to God. What do you have to lose? You probably aren't doing too well on your own. When others cause mayhem, they are acting out on their own fears and insecurities. You become their scapegoat. You can bet they are not starting their morning with prayer and meditation. Only you can fill that hole in your emotional energy. Can you spend time alone with yourself? Are you satisfied with your behavior? The only part of the world that you can improve is you. Make a difference in one person's life today. Knowledge is useless if you are not a kind loving soul. Acceptance kills fears and anxieties. See your past as lessons. Gratitude will lower your expectations. Nothing good can come from making the choice to do bad. TYJ

May 8

Just for today, embrace, respect and honor your feelings. A healthy feeling is full of love, respect and inspiration. An unhealthy feeling is full of fear, resentment and "why do people treat me so poorly?" In other words, playing the victim. What you focus on you will bring into your life, so why would you spend 1 second fretting about what others think of you? Dwell on what God thinks of you because when the time comes, He will be the one judging you, not them. Be comfortable with your weirdness for it is who you are. You do matter for your kindness will leave an impression on others. Find joy in the fact that you have overcome your shortcomings of self-satisfaction, intolerant smugness, lazy complacency and the refusal to admit mistakes. If you are not there yet, give some thought to running out of time before you can make the choice to become a better person. If you are waiting for the right time, it is now. Learn to thank God for the good and the bad while learning from the lessons God is teaching you for your poor choices. When you do decide to improve your life, you will have learned a powerful lesson. It is called peace and serenity. Look for the real people who react out of kindness and love because they have found the secret. TYJ

May 9

Worry ends when Faith begins. Tell your anxiety that your God is bigger than The Darkside. Uncertainty, either real or imagined is a form of negative prayer for you are telling God that you don't think He can handle your difficulties. With morning prayer and meditation, you learn that people who stand up for themselves are not irresponsible, irrational or selfish. Let God help you to loosen the restraints of control that the Enemy has put on your beliefs. Choose to hang with people who can bring you into the Light. If you are stuck in the same predicament month after month, you are not learning your lesson. Are you wondering why your life is always negative? If you treat others with disrespect, the law of the Universe will have your encounter with others unpleasant. Stop blaming God because it is your insolent actions that are causing your problems. Make the choice to remain calm in all situations for God will be with you through the good and the bad. TYJ

May 10

You get well 1 small step at a time. Start with getting rid of your overwhelming shameful feelings that you are not good enough. Stop trying to control others' opinions by allowing them to be who they are, and you will then be able to be yourself. You will no longer have to force situations to work out the way you think they should. You will view your day as a new beginning and not have to look back at the broken pieces of your life. All those years ago need to remain your bygones. Put them in your God box and stop revisiting your past every day. Appreciate the new you. Make your inner peace your daily priority. Focus on what lies ahead by transitioning from a negative purpose in life to a vibrant positive spiritual being. You realize what is important and what is not. Not there yet? Do not give up. Start your day with morning prayer and meditation. Stay focused on keeping your Spiritual life strong. Your hardest test will be to be kind to unkind people. Be patient for with God's direction, everything will be okay. A beautiful heart will bring joy back into your life. At all times seek God's assistance for He will provide emotional encouragement while you navigate through all your problems. Thank Him when you make it through the tough times by showing gratitude every day, for in God's eyes, you will always be enough. TYJ

May 11

Be cautious of people whose actions do not match their words. They will tell you what you want to hear and then do what is best for themselves. Nothing else matters. There are people out there who keep their word. They put others 1st over their own needs. They find themselves by freely doing service for others knowing they may not receive anything in return and never let negative people change who they are. With morning prayer and meditation, they have learned to love themselves unconditionally and do not need to be mean to others. To them, every day is a new beginning. They have no worry of what others think of them. They know that nothing in life is permanent and can go with the flow when situations change. They know they hold the solution to all their problems. Ladies and gentlemen, this is called peace and serenity. They have put Light in their Darkness and have love in their hearts. For those still living on the Darkside, may you make the choice to join the real people today. TYJ

May 12

If you choose to look back at your past, do so with gratitude. Most things did not turn out the way you planned they would. Reflect on how you tried to control everything so your life would be perfect. Ask yourself, how did that work out for you? Each day you need to allocate time to your own serenity, with morning prayer and meditation, reading, going for nature walks, eating healthy foods and drinking lots of water. Know that you deserve self-care. Your new busy is spending time with people you care about. You realize that God has removed the pain, difficulties and fears that our bad choices caused us. He has replaced them with happiness and peace of mind. Contentment starts with you for it is an inside job. You are aware you are going to make it because God will arm you with the strength and security to handle all situations. Tell God what you need and thank him for taking care of it. True peace and serenity is when nothing worked out the way you envisioned them. You had a minor slip of trying to control things. Spiritual growth is when doing your nightly inventory, you can still thank Him for a beautiful day knowing you survived the day with courage and grace. TYJ

May 13

People mistakenly give us the power to make them happy or miserable. The Darkside targets their mind with lies. Their life is filled with pain and suffering. They see the worst in every situation. Everything upsets them. They worry about what everyone thinks of them. They live in total Darkness questioning why we have found the Light and are so happy and positive while their life sucks. Karma does play a part in this. They don't realize they make the choice to play the part of the victim. Nothing is ever good enough and it is our fault that their life is a mess. Most of us used to be there. The only thing we are doing differently is we have made the decision to take responsibility for our own happiness. We start our day with morning prayer and meditation, seeking God's will for us. We have learned to get out of our misery by helping others to get out of theirs. One day it just all made sense. We smile because we are proud of the person we have fought to become. God heard our prayers and saw our tears. Today we have the faith that He will be there for us. To handle our life situations no matter how large or troublesome. We have learned from our mistakes and turned them into lessons. We make the choice to fill our days with good thoughts, kind people and happy moments. TYJ

May 14

When you are in frame of mind that nothing anyone else does is right or good enough, it is essential that you look at what is bothering you. Be grateful for your messy screwed up past for it made you who you are today. God wants to rock your world so make the decision to let Him. The Darkside can no longer harm you if you do not allow Him to control your thinking for your thoughts are powerful. God knows you are not perfect and sometimes you lose your temper. Come to the realization that not everything you think comes from God. Apologize, make your amends and vow to do better the next time your expectations are not met. You can change your attitude to a positive, grateful life by starting your day with morning prayer and meditation. Good, bad or indifferent the people in your life are meant to be there. It is very important to watch their actions, so you know their purpose for they are here to help you find your Spirituality or to teach you a lesson. What you did in the past cannot be changed. There is no, "if only you had done it differently." You did it, live with it. Stop blaming others. Make the decision, right now, to start the new chapter of your Spirituality. TYJ

May 15

Because of my faith in God, I now understand my needs and have received the courage to be myself. I truly appreciate the healing that has taken place. Being a child of God, I no longer fear tomorrow or feel guilt or shame about my past. Worry, anxiety, anger and depression no longer control my life. Believing in The Sermon on the Mount, I have concluded that my spiritual life contains 2 feelings. Love which is God-centered and that all other feelings are derived from fear which is self-centered. When your negative mind is controlled by the Darkside and your world is moving too fast and filled with chaos, do the same as you would with your computer when it is not working. Turn it off or hit the pause button. If you base your beliefs on God as you understand Him which is a spiritual program of action, not thinking. There are those who have strong beliefs that their God is the only one true God and they therefore cannot accept our God as we understand Him theory. I clearly enjoy my time spent each morning in prayer, healing and meditation. The 2nd most important part of my day is spent in fellowship with my many friends. People who truly love you would never destroy your peace of mind. Pay attention to their actions. TYJ

May 16

When praying for others, pray for them to have the strength to endure what life will throw at them today. I read several prayer and meditation books each morning. Not one of them said to worry to be stressed over life situations. They talked about trusting God and to seek His will for today and not to spend any time trying to figure things out on your own. You do know that others must suffer the pain of their past deeds. You cannot take away the emotional experience from anyone for past selfish behaviors they may have committed. Karma is stronger than any power you may think you possess. God has the power to change situations but not what is due to you. Do you want to enjoy good in your life? Then start by doing good for others. If you want love you have to be loving. If you want to acquire comfort you have to comfort others. If you want to experience understanding, start with understanding others. It is not rocket science. Make the choice to be kind and loving today. Selfish individuals do not get this simple part of recovery. TYJ

May 17

At the end of today, look at how your day went. If you started your day with morning prayer and meditation, seeking God's will for you, things had the possibility of working out for the best. Maybe not your best but someone's best. If you have learned to be grateful for the success and happiness of others, you have come a long way. If it is still all about you, then as we say, "Keep coming back until the miracle happens." And we will continue praying for you. God is bigger than any problem you had today unless you try to do it on your own. Then the possibilities of things not working out will increase immensely. You will be pushed to the brink of your endurance to teach you a lesson, causing you to seek Him. Remember but do not dwell on what you went through. Forgive others but do not forget because there are some nasty, selfish people out there still living in the Darkness. Seek out people who have suffered life to the greatest paramount degree of unhappiness for they possess the highest potential of understanding. TYJ

May 18

Let go of things you cannot control. That starts with other people. You have no sway over and in how people are going to treat you. You learn to direct the course of action by how and in what way you respond to the conditions that others treat you. In the past, I replied with rage and resentments when I perceived that you were not treating me the way I thought you should. I felt false power when people recoiled in fear. My reward to all of this was loneliness because no one wanted to be around me for my rage was an addiction. I thought I was doing the right things by controlling my fits of rage. I would keep them inside so people would not behave in fear. There would come that time when someone would do something either at the grocery store or driving that would set me off. The pressure cooker had reached its boiling point and I would explode. How simple it is to talk calmly about what is bothering me instead of stuffing my feelings. Little Jimmy wanted to be heard for his fears were real to him. My parent's solution to life situations was, "stop crying or I'll give you something to cry about" or "big boys don't cry." It was through morning prayer and meditation that I learned the flawed behavior can be unlearned. Life can be difficult, but you are not chained to your past. By doing God's will, I learned a new way for little Jimmy to express himself. It would please me if you would think of doing it this way or how about, "what would you like to do today?" life is best when you spend it with people you love. Don't waste your time looking for someone who can buy you the most stuff for true peace comes from the inside. TYJ

May 19

People who do not see an issue with their actions are not going to change. Worrying about them is understandable. Praying for them to see the errors in their life and leaving them in God's hands is a better use of your time. Waiting for them to make a simple apology is difficult when they are stuck in their childish ways. Immature people feel more comfortable holding on to a resentment for the rest of their lives when a simple, "I am sorry" could patch things up right now. There's an old Chinese proverb: "your current situation is not your final destination." Sometimes we have to look hard, but we can always see good in others. When you find something good, let them know. They may be hurting so badly inside that a kind word may be just what they needed to hear. They may not have God in their life to relieve their pain and give them an ease of feeling from distress. There are rewards for helping others. If you want to be loved, comforted and understood you must love, comfort and understand others so you can become a Channel of God's peace. TYJ

May 20

Life is meant to be enjoyed one day at a time without complaining, living with anxieties or being negative. Be grateful for the difficult people in your life. They can serve as role models that you do not want to emanate along with serving as opportunities for growth. With morning prayer and meditation, you can work on finding your Higher Power. I asked myself, "how do I find this power and where is it located?", it is inside you. Not trusting in or having a source of power is not the end of the world. You start where you are at. I started with the voice in my head called my conscious and used a spiritual advisor. It took me over 20 years to come up with a God of my understanding who was not a punishing God. I do not do religion. I had to learn to love myself enough to want to change. Saying I was sorry all the time without change is manipulation. I became a better person by taking baby steps and each day I would work on being better than I was the day before. If you trust or don't trust that this will work, you are correct. You create your own world by what your opinions and beliefs are. Start and end your day filled with gratitude and I will guarantee the hours in between will be blessed with abundances. You make the choice to live in Darkness or in the Light. TYJ

May 21

Our actions and words affect others. Be cautious of what you say or do for it is not always about you. God is not impressed with your good intentions or your marvelous achievements. Your purpose in life is to bestow others with kindness, compassion and love. Being double minded blocks you from the sunlight of the Universe. There are those who find this hard to believe. With morning prayer and meditation, God will help you to see the good in others and to be happy with who you are today. Not all people will understand your spiritual journey. Since it is yours and not theirs, you do not need to apologize for it. Choose to let God use you as a vessel to do good for others without seeking reward for your reliable behavior or for finding your way out of your past destructive world. Pray that you never go back to the Darkside. Today you know God has given you health, love, gracious family members and loving friends. Choose to be grateful for the wonderful life God has bestowed upon you. TYJ

May 22

Stress and anxiety come from living to please others. Learn to respond to assisting others with a positive attitude. Aiding others needs to be a pleasure and not, "you have to do this." Contributing to others may seem strange at first so start your morning with prayer and meditation by learning to figure out your mind starting with small habits. Talk to yourself about wanting to help others, reading positive information that affirms your new outlook on life. Hang with people who believe what you want to believe. You are not in this alone so start by putting everything in God's hands today and He will turn your fears into security. Get out of the rut of self-inflicted pain or the abuse of others. Take the time today to build for a stronger tomorrow. Know that God will bring you through any storm you are passing through today. Spend time with nature, finding out who you are and what your needs are. Set up boundaries and do not lower them for anyone. TYJ

May 23

Create a life that feels morally desirable on the inside rather than one that looks advantageous on the outside. It is important that you are satisfied with yourself. Others are going to think what they want to no matter what you do. Your true friends will see the beauty in your soul and not judge you by your outer appearance. We all have had unacceptable experiences in our lives. Do not let panic spoil your lesson for loss of courage is a learned behavior. Keep your life simple by having a firm belief in the reliability that God will remove your fears so you can get on with your blessings for today. Because of bad choices from the past, which caused an inferior quality of life, can now be turned into ultimate good. Be careful of your thoughts when you are alone. It helps to keep your mind positive by starting your day with morning prayer and meditation and by letting God into your life to provide you with the courage to start your life over so you can have peace of mind by realizing that everything will turn out okay. Do not block your blessings by seeking revenge for others negative behavior. The Darkside uses anxiety to decrease your trust in God and limit your victories. Forgive, believe in the reliance of God for He will bring them their just dues with karma. TYJ

May 24

Don't focus on what is wrong in your life. Find something positive because what you concentrate on you will bring into your life. If negativity is always the center of your attention, you will only see doom and gloom. Profound insights are to be found by studying the wisdom of a Spiritual journey. Your purpose in life is not to be filled with anger and remorse. If you find something that excites you, follow it for it will bring you out of your path of Darkness to the Light. Prayer used to be the last thing that entered my mind when I didn't know what to do. Today along with meditation, it is the 1st thing I do every morning. Not everything requires action right now. I observe situations to get a better understanding of what is required of me. I also asked myself some pertinent questions. Will my choice hurt anyone? Is it ugly or good? Is it a right or wrong course of action according to the laws of the Universe (karma)? I will only make choices that I can live with. Happy are we when we stop complaining and are grateful for the little things in life. We do not need additional stuff. Essentially our journey and effort require us to acquire increased amounts of love and kindness. TYJ

May 25

It is not selfish to love and take care of yourself. Make your happiness a priority for it is a necessity. Above all make kindness a lifestyle. Your inner beauty will be presented by the way you treat others. Have a gracious soul. You may not have it all together today for on your own you are not strong. With morning prayer and meditation, you ask God to join you today and you become powerful for He will provide as you proceed on your journey. You are all works in progress. Be tough enough to walk away from any bad choices you may have made in the past. With God in your life, you will make improved choices today. There are no perfect mates out there so stop looking. Find someone who makes you laugh, and you will have plenty of outstanding memories. You can form one perfect relationship and that one is with God; may you seek Him now. Things will improve as soon as you have learned your lesson. Your part is to be kind and loving to others. Say thank you. Admit when you are wrong for you do have flaws so work on becoming a better person each day. You can never go back and change situations your bad behavior caused. You can make amends and make better choices next time. TYJ

May 26

Not everyone is meant to be in your future. Some people are just passing through to teach you a lesson in life. If they treat you badly it's not because you are a bad person. People who are free from mental disorders do not go around hurting others. They are the ones who chose to live in the Darkside with hate, anger and anxieties. With morning prayer and meditation, you can put yourself in a free from tension state of mind. If you lose this relaxed feeling during the hectic part of your day, stop and take time to compose yourself and get back on track. In everything you do today do your finest. The action of excelling will help you to enjoy happiness and give you a feeling of accomplishment. You are at your best when you are doing what you want to do and not seeing it as you must do it. Envision your life as doing God's work. When doing your nightly inventory, take time to look at something from your past that you can clean up to make room for something good that can happen in your life. Clean up your mistakes or bad choices from today by choosing to make and amend that has been eating away at you or start by paying off old debts. Make room for God to send you a new resource. Life can be hard. Be delighted you were given the option to become a better person. TYJ

May 27

Anger is a feeling that makes your mouth work faster than your brain. God hears your prayers and feels your pain. He understands when you are overwhelmed, exhausted and lost faith in Him that He can work things out. Do not throw in the towel. Trust Him to get you through this. He knows it is tough being in a one-sided relationship. You feel like you have been destroyed mentally. With morning prayer and meditation, take time to heal your inner child and quit living in a shame-based world of judging yourself so harshly for if that person truly loves you, they will not try to destroy you mentally. The hardest lesson you will learn is to stop controlling everything in your life. Learn to let things happen the way and when they are going to happen. It is in God's time, not yours. Your life will become so much simpler if you can learn this one lesson. God cannot undo the bad choices you made in the past. Start today by making one good choice without shame because nothing ever works out for you. May you seek His guidance now. TYJ

May 28

Letting go of a toxic person is a major step towards being happier. Turning it over to God doesn't imply you stopped caring. It signifies you stopped trying to force others to. Pray that you gain the knowledge that any pain you have may not be all your fault. You are responsible for your own growth and healing. With morning prayer and meditation, you will feel God's Light surround you. May home kindle your soul and faith abound in you. Major hurts become wisdom for the future. With God's guidance, your suffering will turn into laughter, and you will gain the knowledge to make better choices in the future. May God's goodness inspire you to go with the flow, make sense of your life and bring peace and gratitude into your world. If you spend your time judging others, you will be filled with anger and unhappiness for they will never meet your expectations. By working on being a better person, you will count your blessings. Be kind to others and let go of what you can't control. Listen to your heart and pray for a productive day. TYJ

May 29

The only limits you have are the restrictions you set for yourself. The strongest people are the ones who have had the hardest life. When you first start looking at yourself and realize that you are the problem, can be the easiest part of change. The most difficult part is making the effort to seek God and ask for His assistance. The pains you go through in life will keep repeating themselves until you reach out and are capable of change. When that feeling of hopelessness sets in, turn to God through prayer and meditation and receive His comfort. At first you feel fragile and powerless, but you will achieve serenity with God's strength. Do not give up, keep fighting for your life. For those of us who have gone through this know that life is a lot better on the other side. Have trust in God that everything will work out. Not knowing is the scariest part. You will come into your relationship with God harboring feelings of insecurity, fear and humiliation. Don't be confused, God and others will be there for you. So within, so without. Finding your way out of our self-destruction will be hard but well worth the effort it took to change. Your relationship with God and others will end up being your prize possession. I guide you; you assist me and together we bother support others. TYJ

May 30

When I take the time to get rid of resentments, forgive others and started to pay off my debts, I am then ready to start on my journey of being happy, joyous and free. By practicing morning prayer and meditation, I will continue my gratifying journey for I cannot learn from my mistakes if I spend all my time denying that I have made any. I am not a perfect individual; therefore, I make errors in judgment. I will continue to take nightly inventory with one goal in mind, to become a better person than I was yesterday. It took me a long time to reach the total darkness that my life had ascended to. I pray that it will not take as long to see the transformation of my life to doing good for others and serving the God of my understanding. I have learned to trust God especially when I am uncertain of where I am headed. Part of that is knowing which voice I am listening to. God is the soft gentle voice. Today the Darkness must get me to believe a lie in order to get me to perform his evil exploits. The Enemy can only promise you stuff. He cannot offer you any help with getting better. TYJ

May 31

Learn to accept what is, let go of what was and gain faith in what will be. For those who are new to this Spiritual life, hope and anxiety cannot reside in the identical location for a similar instant while gaining knowledge that this stuff works. Choosing which one stays will be the best you can wish for. Wanting the world to be a better place to live in starts with you. With morning prayer and meditation, concentrate on letting go of the past. When fear or anxiety set in, may you know that it is time to pause and pray for God's guidance to cut out any negativity. Calmness and anxiety cannot exist in an equal timeframe. Spend time with positive people who can help you with your new definition of love, kindness and grace. Just for today, make the concession that your heart be joyous, and your mind filled with God's love. Your body free of illness and allow your day to be overflowing with gentleness, expressing the possibilities that you respect and appreciate yourself unconditionally without reservation. TYJ

June 1

Today is a gift from God to you, so enjoy it. I know I am a blessed friend who enjoys giving, expecting nothing in return. I love me for who I am so don't judge me too harshly. I do know that others can only see me at the same level they see themselves. Today I will walk away from anyone who does not respect me or see my self-worth. My life is filled with love, honesty, respect and a faith in God. I will not force anything for my spirituality allows me to see what is meant for me. I will be a friend who encourages others to do their best. I give to others when they need help because there will come the day when I need help. I work at not letting my emotions be my decision maker. Through morning prayer and meditation, I ask God for guidance because His vision for today is a lot better than mine. I look for people who are real, not fake. Every night I forgive anyone who hurt me. May you find the same peace and healing in your life and may God protect you and your loved ones and keep you safe today. TYJ

June 2

Just in case you needed to hear this today, you are not a failure or a waste of space. You are loved and wanted. Through morning prayer and meditation, make the choice to change the shortcomings in your life that you deem as undesirable. Changing your outsides must start with changing your insides. Feelings of self-worth must start on the inside before you can portray it on the outside. Be proud of the fact that there is no one else in the world like you. God made you different for a reason. Find out what it is. You can make a difference in your life and that of others. You can do it; I believe in you. Use your voice to stand up for yourself and prove to the Universe that you do have values. With guidance from abuse, trust the journey you are on. The storm is over, peace will prevail in your life. You are safe in the arms of God. Do all the good for others that you can. Love them from your heart all the time, not only when they can do good for you. Your struggles will be turned into victories. TYJ

June 3

Turn down the volume on the voice that shames and judges you. You have made bad choices in the past based on information that at the time made perfect sense. I had no idea the Enemy was putting suggestions in my head that were meant to destroy me both mentally and physically. You do not have to stay hostage to your past. Stop the "could of's, should of's and would of's". They are self-imposed downers that the Darkside uses to keep playing on your mind of how bad you were. Starting today, with morning prayer and meditation, make plans to forget the past and start a new chapter in your life. There are going to be days that Karma will bite you in the butt because of bad choices from your past. They will not last. You made the choices so live with the consequences. Do not let them ruin your future. Karma is a cosmic law and there is nothing you can do to stop it. Know this, what you are going through is preparing you for your new exciting life. Seek guidance from God in all matters, starting with right now and I promise you your days will get better. TYJ

June 4

Shaming and judging yourself is feeding the disease that your Enemy wants you to live in. your mind will be the toughest place to escape from for your Darkside wants you living in the negativity of the loud chatty monkey voice. With morning prayer and meditation, you can learn to let go, living without external control. Surrender today and live restriction free. Stress or joy are both choices so choose wisely. It is imperative that you receive the gift of calmness. Not everyone is going to see your worth. Do not devalue yourself for the past broken pieces and terrible choices for they are valuable lessons. The gentle voice says you are a good person, and you are loved. Of all the blessings, both spiritual and material that God will bestow upon you, peace of mind will be your greatest possession. From your friends that will be loyalty and honesty along with a loving soul who will respect you for who you are and will take pride in helping you to become the loving person that God sees you as. TYJ

June 5

You are a strong, capable person who respects yourself and others. Be cautious of people who induce you to react on your Darkside with fear or anger and then play the role of poor me when you go there. It is not important what others say or do to you. What is crucial is how you react. So, stop worrying about what others think about you. Let the All-Knowing Father handle the Karma. You will receive different messages from the Universal Life Force throughout your day. Write them down and piece them together for that will be God's answer to whatever questions you may be asking. Starting your day with constructive optimism along with morning prayer and meditation will improve how you react to others. Just for today, let go of how you thought this day would go and enjoy what God has sent you. The Gentle voices says you are not alone. Enjoy staying positive. If anything overwhelms you today, stop and ask God for assistance. Rest if you are tired. Make a call when loneliness rears its ugly soul. Eat something healthy. TYJ

June 6

Everyone is struggling with something. Some worse than others. I have noticed that those who start their day with morning prayer and meditation have a more informed perception on how to handle theirs by calming their mind and making improved choices, hence effective outcomes. This is not rocket science. Acceptance plays a big part in this. Don't be so quick to judge others. If you find yourself unhappy and fearful, you are doing something wrong. My guess is that you are spending your time analyzing others. God is not hiring. Fixers are always looking for someone or something to improve. I say spend your time working on yourself for you are the only person you can improve upon. Give up on any thoughts of controlling others, it will not work out. Affirm your own goodness and be as one with a loving God. If you must deal with a toxic person today, do so with caution by 1st seeking God's guidance and things will have an exceptional chance of falling into place. TYJ

June 7

I pray I never forget the mornings I did not want to get out of bed. I recall what a struggle it was to make it through another day. Loneliness would cause me to reach out to toxic people. My self-worth was nonexistent and there was no peace of mind. I looked for happiness in all the wrong places, thinking the next relationship was going to fix me. The new car did nothing to relieve my pain. I suffered through 22 years of pain, misery and depression. Then one day I came across the prayer of Saint Francis and my world changed. The next day I started my morning with prayer and meditation and all the rage, fear and depression was lifted. True happiness can only be achieved with a Higher Power, someone other than you yourself. Accept where you are at today with a grateful heart and the Universe will supply the miracle needed for recovery. Today I have peace of mind and am emotionally calm and truly enjoy helping others find their way out of the Darkside. Stop looking out there. It is inside of you. Forget the competition to be better than anyone else. Just work on being better than you were yesterday. TYJ

June 8

You are at peace with yourself, and you acknowledge your needs. If you need boundaries, set them. If anyone gets upset because they no longer profit by your lack of guidelines, so be it. Set them anyway. Starting today, life is about your happiness. You no longer conform to the ways of the Darkside. You need to take a day for yourself. You are not a failure if you don't get everything done. If you are addicted to more, as in negative thoughts, ice cream, cookies, pie, overworking or lying on the couch, stop rationalizing and justifying your behavior of occurring adverse effects. Switch your dependency to more fruit, vegetables, protein, exercise, being outdoors and time spent with your Higher Power in morning prayer and meditation. Just for today, love who you are. Do not wish to be anyone else for God created you for a purpose. It starts with becoming devoted to God and letting Him help you cope with your daily life by feeding the brains reward center with His love. Become enthusiastically devoted to helping others. TYJ

June 9

Get realigned with your inner voice. Put your trust in the serenity, calm and tranquility your God provides. When I first started my journey towards spirituality, I did not possess anything near the God of my understanding that I am in touch with today. I was defiant, selfish, self-centered, self-delusional, self-seeking, and full of fear and self-pity. Other than those defects, I thought my life was just peachy. Along with being defensive and suspicious, I was filled with condemnation. I saw others as my problem. An untruth is still a distortion even though my perception (Darkness) had me believing otherwise. With all those imperfections to overcome, finding a Power greater than myself was not an easy task. That loud chatty monkey voice would discredit anything the soft Inner voice would convey to me. I had to start with stepping outside of myself and realizing that I was not the center of the Universe. I saw it work for others so I started with a belief, a glimmer of hope that it would work for me. For anyone new to this finding a Spiritual life, it starts with a loving, kind inner peace within you, not anything materialistic. Practice being calm throughout the day in all situations and a God of your understanding will appear. Remember the Darkside can only offer you stuff. Today I have the faith needed to trust in God. May you find yours. TYJ

June 10

You make the choice to let serenity flow into your life. You feel appreciated and give to others without strings attached. Surround yourself with people who react in the same manner. Selfish, self-centered people only call when they need something. Take time to observe the people around you. It will mean sitting quietly watching their actions, not listening to their con game. A real fraud has the unique ability to say what they think you need to hear. Rarely do they think that their actions speak loudly for they are too busy presenting themselves as God's gift to the Universe. When you depend upon others to make you feel significant there will always be something substantially missing in your life. It is your own special decision-making core values that endorse you. With morning prayer and meditation, let your inner voice help you to legitimize your accountability and make you unique. Just for today, take the time to provoke someone's Darkness with your Light. Be a shining example of God's goodness. Do not agree with the fear and dominion of the Darkside. If you do anything today to make your life better, you will be ahead of those who choose to do nothing to better themselves. TYJ

June 11

You meet new opportunities without fear and will not be intimidated. Pay attention to your thinking for it will tell you everything you need to know about yourself. When confronted with a life situation, what is the 1st thing you do? If you have been paying attention to what is being said every morning through prayer and meditation, you will say, "God, you got this." You know that God is all loving and will work everything out for the best of all humanity. It may not be the best for you but remember, not all-inclusive outcomes are about you. If the first thing you do is jump into your worry mode and let fear and anxiety set in, you have not learned a thing. Once again, love is God-centered, fear is self-centered. Not everyone you meet today will be trustworthy. Observe their actions. Do not let any negative thoughts control you today. Unpleasant emotions causing pain and compulsive behavior caused by uncertain outcomes are negative feelings. Be the reason people want to change. Peace and serenity are the consequences benefited from positive thinking. Your choice. Do you grow weeds or flowers? TYJ

June 12

Today is going to be a joyful day. You have chosen not to let the failures of your past upset you or your worries about the future cause you to react with feelings of fear and anxiety. In the past, God has had to cause to you feel uncomfortable to get your attention. You need to realize that just because you are working on becoming a better person, not all your life situations are going to be perfect. All we can promise you is that you will make intelligent choices when the s*** hits the fan. There will still be fall out for past retribution from the Cosmic Truth of Karma. With morning prayer and meditation, you have stopped wasting time caring what others think about you. You trust your instincts to do what is important for you and will do it with kindness and love, using God's will for you as your guide. When at all possible, you will avoid people who mess with your head and upset you or selfishly want you to make them your priority. Helping others is not meant to give them an opportunity to take advantage of you. Just for today, you will listen to your inner voice your conscience. You are not perfect; you will make mistakes. Do not blame others, for the bad outcome of any decision you made for you are the problem. Miscalculations will hurt. Time will heal all wounds. Your peace will be found in the stillness of your soul. TYJ

June 13

You feel relaxed, surrounded by love and will make things happen by putting yourself as a number 1 person to mend today. You cannot assist others if you are spiritually bankrupt. You can only make a different for them if they want the benefits of guidance from a Higher Power. Pay attention to their actions because their words only prove who they are attempting to create a delusion of being. Offer support without thoughts of reward for your benefits will be from the giving not from the receiving. Happiness is an inside job so today do 1 thing that makes you delighted and forgive 1 person who did you wrong not because they merit it, you will gain peace of mind. Your Darkside is out to destroy you but will settle for diverting your attention from your Higher Power. This morning, start your day with prayer and meditation by choosing to react with kindness and appreciation focusing your attention on others with unselfish words and by showing love, tolerance and understanding. Stay strong and never give up the fight. TYJ

June 14

Forgive yourself and others. You are in charge of your life. Just for today, direct your attention on what you can change. To the outer world you may appear strong and independent while on the inside you are inhibited and fearful. You focus on how you think others want you to be like. Your love is conditional based on how others treat you. You are forever thinking and pushing others for favorable outcomes. You are critical of others and blame them for your feelings of inadequacy and your inability to deal with life situations. You are overwhelmed with feelings of not being enough so to compensate for those feelings you become selfish and self-centered. Through morning prayer and meditation, you can overcome these defects. You can change your standard line of, "I am fine, leave me alone. Why do you want to know? You don't care no one does." Our new line will change to, "life is great, God has been good to me. I have everything I need. I have friends who love me for who I am." This starts with you wanting to change to becoming a better person. You may not realize this but anyone with a negative attitude stands out in a crowd. It is time to come out of the beacon of Darkness and into the Light. God has never ever told you to be critical or judgmental of others. Why do you continue to allow the Darkside to control your mind? TYJ

June 15

You view your childhood without shame, opening your soul through your inner child knowing you can now handle criticism with ease. Your mind is going to tell you that you are worthless, no good and will never amount to anything. As a young child this was how I reacted to the message my father gave me. Today I know he was hurting, and we know emotionally distressed people wound others. In relationships, I unconsciously looked for women who were emotionally abusing. I would look for things from the Darkside to ease my pain. It was my perception that I did not deserve anything better. Through morning prayer and meditation, I came to realize I was worth the effort to become a better person. I looked at how I treated others and took responsibility for my part in relationships admitting that I was a toxic individual who hurt others because I was agitated. I had to stop rationalizing and justifying my behavior and face the fact that I was responsible for changing my life today. TYJ

June 16

You have confidence, rejoicing in your abilities. You thank God for the new person you have become. Be an example of God's love and kindness. You are not going to change anything by giving us your opinion. When you see others doing random acts of kindness, thank them for their unselfish behavior. Start your day with morning prayer and meditation, don't wait for your day to go bad and then start praying for God to help you. Bring him with you wherever you go. God gave you a free will to do whatever you want. You also need to be able to accept the consequences of your actions. Just for today, set a goal of staying away from unnecessary drama. Choose to be a part of the peace and serenity that you deserve. Look at the parts of your day that you were unlovable. At the end of your day thank God for any goodness you were able to send to others. At some point in your life, you really need to take a sincere look at your shortcomings vowing to do better tomorrow. Your Darkside wants you believing that you are good enough. He wants to ruin your day by promising you stuff and it is the others who need to change. Not so. It starts with you. Only God can mend your shattered dreams. TYJ

June 17

You are happy with your circle of healthy friends you have in your life today as you begin to establish your limits and boundaries. Make the choice to be around people who respect and understand you. You have been told not to judge others, but this is the one time you can take their inventory. How else will you know who the winners are? Do they support the life you are choosing to live? Have a purpose in life and express your love of God. Do not do good to impress others so they will applaud you. Through morning prayer and meditation, you put your family, health, fears and security in God's hands today. There is nothing that you and God cannot handle together. God will provide your needs but for your own good, He may hold back on your wants. Keep an open mind and seek peaceful solutions with your everyday adventures. Deal with any anger daily. Never react with a rageful heart. Anger turned inward will cause depression. Work on staying calm through all of life situations. Do not let anger punish you by destroying everything. When you get angry, they win. TYJ

June 18

You will make good out of any situation you face today. Your involvement will produce winners. Things will happen that you did not ask for. The people who hurt you the most made you the admirable person you are today. Your thoughts evolve into forming your Universe, so why would you think negative ones? With morning prayer and meditation, make the choice to let God be by your side. You know you got this. You are no longer here to choose drama and anxiety. You have made effective decisions on who is desirable for your peace of mind. You have done the work required to improve your own self-worth. You are no longer held prisoner to any situation you cannot control or change and have learned to put those in your God Box. I pray that God will take away the anger in others and give them the peace of mind He has afforded me. TYJ

June 19

Sometimes it is hard to move on. You spend your time looking at other's shortcomings instead of looking at yourself. Once you make the decision to change, you realize it was the best choice you ever made. People disliking us is not a thing. Their ego instills fears in them when you are growing in God's love and understanding. You have stopped looking out there for your happiness. There are those who will never be pleased no matter how kind or filled with love you are. Sometimes life is too short to start your day with the broken people of yesterday. You have let go of the need to be loved by others and have started the process of loving yourself. Those of you with the darkest past are going to shine the brightest with your newfound love of God. With morning prayer and meditation, you can make the choice to be positive or negative. Choosing to be positive helps you to see your blessings and to view your problems with a strong attitude. Staying negative causes you to feel inadequate because all you see is the unacceptable behavior in your life. It takes more work to be miserable than happy. Stop arguing. TYJ

June 20

Surround yourself with people who make you laugh along with treating you with kindness and respect. Forget the bad, focus on the positive for your happiness comes from the results of a better quality of life. Selfish people cannot empathize with others for they can only understand your mental impressions based on their ability to interpret your thinking. Like all feelings, it will not remain permanent because of choices you will have made. With morning prayer and meditation, you have a better chance of being blessed rather than stressed. Putting your faith in God will relieve your worries and anxieties. He will make a way for you. Put your trust in His timing. If a door does not open, do not fret about it or force your way in for it may be the wrong time or may never be right for you. Most of your bad times were a result of doing whatever you wanted because seeking God's will was never an option that presented itself to you at that time. Make the choice to be in touch with your inner silence for you will gain a technique to maintaining a daily routine of being kind and loving. TYJ

June 21

Appreciate the people who treat you right and love how you feel when you are around them. Pray for those who do not for life is too short to be anything but happy. You oversee your destiny. With morning prayer and meditation, God will help you to respond to living life on life's terms. Because of bad choices made in the past, there will be awkward, painful predicaments you will need help responding to so stop fighting the people God sends to help you. You may not be able to choose the cards you are dealt but you can embrace how you react to them. God awarded you with a free will. Doing whatever you want causes results and conditions that may not be pleasant to you, or others so choose your actions wisely. God uses pain to teach you your lessons so learn from them, and your assignments will not need to keep repeating themselves. Take care of your own sweet self, the Universe can handle the rest on its own. TYJ

June 22

Don't allow others to put their limitations on you. Go for it. Be the best you can be. You should never have to convince someone of your worth. If others don't appreciate you, they don't deserve you. Be with people who know the value of your love, kindness and serenity. What is meant to be will be. Your part is to deal with the situation correctly, not how you think it should be. Stop, think about the consequences of your actions for problems are easier to fix now rather than going back to repair the damage of acting out of anger. The Darkside wants you living in anxiety and misery. God only wants what's good for you. Never give up and know your value so you will never have to worry about what others think of you. Hang with people who celebrate you, not just tolerate you. Your freedom is not being dominated by others causing you to live in an emotional state that someone or something is dangerous or threatening. Be cautious of people who are filled with Satan's hate and tell lies about God's children. TYJ

June 23

Each morning you are afforded the opportunity to start a new life for yourself. Do you choose to stay stuck in your old behavior or do you put to become a better person? When you make the choice, God will open new doors for you. You are responsible for the effort; the outcome is in God's hands. You must realize that because of bad choices you made, there may be negative Karma due to you. A bad attitude causes judging, criticizing and blaming others and is a mental handicap that keeps you from enjoying life. Make the choice to see things as truthful as they are, not what you think they should be. If you change your lifestyle starting today, you will change any future karma to the plus side of the ledger. Use the prayer of Saint Francis as your guide. You will not do the prayer perfectly although it will not hurt you to strive for doing the best you can with your morning prayer and meditation. TYJ

June 24

Look to God with morning prayer and meditation, blessing your body with positive thoughts for the power of healing yourself. Listen to soft music and sounds of water for the mastery of serenity. It is imperative that you get in contact with your Higher Power to connect to the influence of the Universe for your purpose in life and to continue your Spiritual Growth in wisdom and love. You are all given the same 24 hours each day. For the people who choose to stay in their old behavior of complaining about everything and everybody, you can be extremely annoying to those who have found the secret to life, which is acceptance and gratitude. Take the time to know who you are, what gives you satisfaction and why certain pieces of information specifically set you off in a fit of anger. You may need to go back to your childhood to find the answer to that one. As spiritual advisors, God may have chosen to give you a tough person to bring out of the darkness. Learn to seek His help with their dark negative side is acting out in defiance and all they can see is everything that is wrong in everybody. Choose to seek God and He will give you the strength to make it through every day. TYJ

June 25

Do not deny your own feelings to make someone else happy. You do matter, let this benefit you. Choose your thoughts carefully by telling yourself that you are a kind loving person who shares those images with another. Do not worry about what the fools think of you. Haters will always hate. Overthinking is not a gift from God. True contentment is your priority, and you will not allow negativity to exist. Trying to be someone else is a way of telling yourself you are not important. Set your sights high by being with the winners exemplifying what they do. Here's the thing, people do not have to like you and you will not let it bother you unless you are one of those selfish self-centered types. Then you need to make the choice to become a better person. By starting your day with morning prayer and meditation, you share where you are at today and forgive yourself for past failures. Learn to follow your dreams by seeking God's guidance and you are less likely to fail. God may choose to not give you everything you desire to teach you patience, humility, trust, a life with meaning and purpose. This comes from the inside. The Darkside can only give you stuff. TYJ

June 26

Pay attention to how each person touches your soul while viewing them with acceptance and gratitude. Everyone needs a friend who will sit with you in silence when words do not work. Your silence with God during morning prayer and meditation is not empty, for answers will come when you are in tune with the Soft Gentle Voice. Be aware of the Loud Chatty Monkey Voice for that is the ugly sounds of the Darkside. Choose to stay in the Light. Cover your family and friends with God's protection today through prayer. Don't ask for a perfect life, go with happy instead for God will give you the strength to deal with your struggles. The richest people have their inner abundance, not money or possessions. Be the individual others need in their life. Today is a good day to make your dreams come true. You are being sent this prayer to help formulate your meditation on the action you will proceed with to become a better person. TYJ

June 27

If you are easily angered, it is because you are off balance. It is never others, God or life situations. It is you who must take responsibility for your actions by changing for the better. You need to stop blaming others for whatever is going on in your life today. Not everything is going to be good because of past Karma. Just for today, look at who you really are, not what your perceptions has you thinking you are. Praise your good points while looking at what you have done that may not be pleasing to God. Start with, if you were angered once today, you are at fault. Work on a plan on how to improve yourself. The despairing version of others that you have created in your mind could be a starting point for your own defects. Do not dwell on any hopeless situations the Darkside has slipped into your thoughts for this is no fairy tale. He wants you spiritually dead. Instead start your day meditating on God's will for you. He wants you to change your thinking from criticism of others to being optimistic. Learn to Love yourself and do good for others. Forgive all transgressions (either real or fabricated) against you. Do no harm to another human being or animal. Choose Faith over fear for God wants you to be successful. TYJ

June 28

Discussions are better than arguments. Heated exchange of opposing views is to find out who is right, and a conversation is to reach a decision or interactive communication with the purpose of finding out what is right rather than thinking your ways is the only way. You may deem them to be unreasonable or self-centered. Not every conversation you are involved in deserves your total energy. There will be times when your serenity and peace of mind is more important. Learn to listen to their point of view with compassion and kindness in your heart. Look at the reality of the subject matter and be willing to change your conception without getting angry for that may lead to a disaster. Take the mature role, learning to love without conditions and caring for others without assumptions. God's will for you is to be loving, honest, respectful and living without lies. God will help you to achieve compassion and empathy. The Darkside can only offer you stuff. Our purpose in life is to help others. If you are not there yet at least put in the effort to stop hurting them. TYJ

June 29

If I am listening to God's guidance I will never have to rationalize or justify my behavior for He will never tell me to lie, cheat, gossip, cheat on or steal. He will ask me to be compassionate to others and not to take on their worries or problems as yours. You may need to let them reach their bottom. You have been through a lot in your life and learned substantially. That is causing you to think you can fix everyone. Spend your time working on yourself. Helping others when asked for advice or counseling, listening with understanding, praying with them and for them. Your joy in life will come from a gracious heart and helping others. All the gold or diamonds in the world will not bring that kind of joy. I can rationalize and justify my s***** behavior with the best of them. You can either rationalize or justify your behavior or you can work on becoming a better person. Changing the world, others or your significant others starts with you. End of conversation. TYJ

June 30

The gap between expectations and reality causes stress. If you lower your anticipations of yourself and others you will lessen the chance of being overwhelmed or irritated. All change in your life starts with your impressions. Make the choice to control your emotions. Your first consideration requires you to see that you are enough. The only way you can attract a stress-free class of friends is to improve your mental health. There are evil people out there controlled by the Darkside who will disrespect you and treat you badly. Not everyone has Faith so let God deal with them for He has this thing called Karma. Teach your children and others you are working with to handle their difficulties with Grace. Do not fix their issues for them, instead help them to become problem solvers. Let people know when they brighten your day. I see God leading people to the program of Spirituality. Do not let them stop short of achieving their goals. We tend to rest on our laurels and take the easier softer way. It is okay to push others to greatness. God will supply the guidance; you need to react. Your final stage of healing is to help others for God has the power to change any situation. Remember, you survived what was supposed to kill you. Thank you, Jesus. TYJ

July 1

Worry serves no purpose. Whatever is going to happen will happen. Give these stress causing situations to God and stop your compulsive behavior of uneasiness and apprehension. 2 years or 2 weeks from now will you remember what caused your anticipation of misfortunate disorders today? Please acquire the ability to choose to let go of everything against for Forces of the Darkside you cannot control. Do not be a fallback plan for someone else for you are worth more than that. With God's guidance you will attract people who see the beauty in your soul, causing you to believe you are a magnificent person deserving of love and intimacy. With morning prayer and meditation, you will receive the gift of everything feeling right. Calmness will enter your life with love, acceptance, being blessed and overcome by feelings of gratitude. TYJ

July 2

Do not try to be perfect for everyone. Be good enough for God, yourself and the people who deserve you. Remember the good times, forgiven the people who treated you poorly with nastiness in their ugly souls but don't forget the lessons learned. A positive attitude will help to create a life worthy of living. Choose to give yourself reasons to improve your spirituality so you can become the kind loving person God intended you to be. If you continue to assign a very strong disapproval or blame of others for your misfortunes, you will forgo any chance of ever being happy. Do not take it personally. Be kind always for it says everything about them and their bad behavior. Sometimes life hurts, give it your best on all occasions. Do not forget to thank God for the greatest comeback of all times for no one can block God's blessings. With God's guidance, grow with love and understanding increasing your belief in and dependence on God, not others, for God will never let you down. TYJ

July 3

Your stress levels are dictated by how you respond to life. Being negative is like sitting on a sharp stick causing yourself unneeded pain and misery. Stop doing that. If you assign condemnation to others for your misfortunes, you will never be happy. Blaming yourself is a little bit better. Listen to that soft gentle voice for it will teach you to live a life of love, kindness, comfort and understanding. Obtain something more to adjust your attitude and lower your stress levels. Assigning responsibility to no one for your unfortunate events is a sign of a healthy lifestyle. Knowledge of past experiences along with processing your past behavior has shown you that being soft, and gentle is an improvement in your lifestyle of being a hard-ass a-hole. With morning prayer and meditation, you can get a leg up on your newer softer version, helping you to relieve yourself of past ignorance on the benefits of serving God and others while leaving the heavy burdens and poor choices of your past behind you. TYJ

July 4

I am living in love when I can see the beauty in another's soul which is the spiritual intellectual energy that causes us to react with emotional turmoil, are calm. Make the choice to remain kind and gentle. The Darkside wants you to lash out. Take responsibility for your actions. Do not under any circumstances blame others because of your shitty behavior. Just for today, I will spread joy rather than negativity. Through morning prayer and meditation, I will release myself of any grudges I may have for others. I choose to be at peace within my world by letting go of the pain caused by any revengeful thinking I may harbor in my soul. I will spend today looking for happiness from within by seeing my world with clarity, observing things as they really are not as I perceive them to be with wishful thinking. I will not project any outcomes. I will show the true happiness in my heart and allow others to do as they wish, knowing full well I have no control over anything they do. I am not responsible for their actions. TYJ

July 5

Music is good for the soul for it helps to heal the hurt, pain and loneliness of yesterdays while bringing back memories of past years. Just don't dwell too long on old hurts for obsessing on the past will serve no useful purpose. Learn to go to your secret place each morning to help with healing old wounds. Take the time to ask God for help with your day, remaining calm in all situations. Make the choice to not overthink which in turn causes overreacting. Do not let the Darkside win. Look for lessons learned knowing that God always made a way for you and your survival. The tiny steps you take each day to become a better person will make big changes in your life over a period. With morning prayer and meditation, look at the days when you judged others instead of understanding them. You have always had a good heart even though you learned lousy methods of dealing with others. Today your goal is to grow in understanding while being compassionate, showing patience and loving others for who they are not who you wanted them to be. You trust in God to work things out for the best for everyone in hopes that He will ignore your selfish needs of wanting what you wanted when you wanted it. Patience. TYJ

July 6

Life is about being happy and taking everything as it comes. Smile and stay positive. Be a good person no matter how others treat you while looking for people who will treat you better. Through morning prayer and meditation, you will learn to keep life real. Choose to remain thankful for God will fill you with love and kindness today, giving you the resources of being generous, and excellent listener and a shoulder for others to cry on. Be the reason people smile when you walk into a room, paying special attention to the selfish, self-centered ones for they are the loneliest. Show compassion, love and courage while carrying on intelligent conversations speaking only the truth. You will be treated poorly by the dishonest. Be honest anyway. Always do good for others, they may not know it was you, do it anyway. Your loving kindness will remain between you and God. TYJ

July 7

People like to hear how marvelous, bold and bright they are. Always tell the truth, having faith that God will work things out. Be proud of who you have become while working on creating a better life for yourself. Do not be dismayed by the troubles of the world for everyday struggles are a part of life. Work on becoming a better person. To those who have harmed you, make sure they have had a total change before you trust them again. Talk is cheap, watch their actions. Be grateful for the lessons learned for not everyone is going to treat you with love and kindness. Your innermost thoughts will take you where God wants you to be. Choose to love intentionally, showing your bright light to all the world around you. The more uncomfortable and painful the world becomes around you, the more you will want to grow in love and understanding. Through morning prayer and meditation, God is telling you to fill the world with inspiration, giving hope to them by seeking God's guidance on all matters. TYJ

July 8

Be generous with praise and cautious with criticism. When you give your word, keep it. Overthinking situations can cause emotionally confused, groundless expectations. Good sound beliefs are okay for it says who you think you are. However, it is your behavior that says who you really are. True happiness is embracing the wonderful person you are becoming. It was never about how much stuff you had. Morning prayer and meditation will help you to reach into the depths of your soul, giving you admittance to finding your truth while helping you to dance to your own music. With God's guidance you can choose to be helpful, happy and free to open your mind to all matters pertaining to you becoming a better person along with sound thinking. You are worth it. Nothing is going to happen today that you and God together cannot handle. Be cautious of selfish people who want you to live your life to improve theirs. TYJ

July 9

Rewrite your brain's tendencies to react calmly and more loving. When someone says you make me so angry, or it was your fault that I got irritated. Remind them that you cannot make anyone angry. It was their choice to react with displeasure. Do not allow anger to live in your house for that is a gift you have received from God with morning prayer and meditation. God will heal what needs to be healed. God gave you free will not to do what you want. He would rather you do what is right. If you have a negative mindset that you are right all the time, you will never be afforded the opportunity to change. Depressed people lack the skills to be considerate of others. Appreciate your close relationships that you have with a few friends who matter to you. Your God is awesome for He has helped you to return from the Darkside. Unlearn the negativity and inaccurate conclusions that you have formed. Today with a strong belief in God along with following His guidance, you have found out who you really are. A kind loving human being. TYJ

July 10

What others think of you is none of your business. Acceptance is the key that lightens the burden of needing others to accept you or from seeking the endorsement of others. With morning prayer and meditation, you need to seek the guidance and approval of God for He is the only person who can and will judge you. True happiness will come from forgiving others, making amends and paying back any ill gained money. Learn to listen to the soft gentle voice and become willing to make the change of loving and opening your soul to the ability to accept what you cannot control along with knowing you deserve the love of God and others. God will continue to love you no matter how many bad choices you make. Your part is to stop making them. With God's loving mercy, you are receiving the ability to heal form past bad situations. Just for today, think success, serenity and happiness. Do not obsess about the future or relive the broken pieces of your past for life goes on with or without your sanction. TYJ

July 11

Always do your best under any circumstances thus avoiding self-judgment, self-condemnation and regret. With morning prayer and meditation, God will help you to find a peaceful solution for every situation you may have conceived to be harmful to your existence. Lower your anxiety by not controlling everybody around you. Telling people you love them is commendable. Whynot go for the fantastic and show them with kindness and deeds. Just for today, focus on self-love thus affording yourself and others true happiness. Not everyone has your comprehension of God so pray for them to find a God of their understanding and how spirituality really works. How you feel about your part in the scheme of things is important. Be real in all your assessments, walk away from drama, focus on the good, get back up one more time than you have failed. Never speak with negativity for your self-talk is important. See God's hand in all your daily routines. Let people know when you are proud of them. TYJ

July 12

Find the courage to express what you want clearly, speaking with integrity and saying what you mean with truth and love to avoid misunderstanding, sadness and drama. Always look for the highest qualities in others along with praying that they will do what is favorable for everyone. Lower your anxiety by letting go of the urge to control the future. Do everyone involved in your life a favor, stop overthinking everything. You did what you did. Nothing is going to change that. You made the choice. Today choose to have peace in your life with morning prayer and meditation being a therapeutic part of recovery and the answer to true happiness. It is not your job to tell others how they should act or feel. Inspire them to do what is best for everyone involved. Urge them to seek God's guidance so they can make sound choices. Be creative. Don't be afraid to try new methods for a lot of your old ideas stopped working a long time ago. Keep striving for a better tomorrow and when tomorrow gets here, do it all over again. It won't take long before your todays are excellent. Listen to the quietness of your soul. TYJ

July 13

Change your attitude by changing your thoughts. Do not look at your life as stressful, call it excitement. Although you may have experienced hard times and failures, you are still here fighting to become better. God did not give birth to you to be a bad example to everyone else. Learn to live life to its fullest. Once you know better you will do better. Until then, fake it until you make it. Never give up. Doing your best also means ceasing to engage in strenuous or stressful activity when you are tired. Do not consider catnapping as wasting time. You don't always have to go, go, go. Your mind and body need time for recovering. Most of your stress comes from how you respond to others. The key is not to react with negative thoughts. When you choose to react in anger, who is your 1st victim? You!!! You do not get to decide what looks good for others. One bad day does not mean you are bad person. Don't allow others to use you. Listen to the problems of others, just don't lose yourself in their situation. Kindness and love are what people need to help with the shifting of attitudes. TYJ

July 14

The way you react to others says a lot about who you are. If you behave poorly, it gives others the opinion that you do not think much of yourself along with the fact that it is what Karma will send back to you. Take all the time you need to learn to address people with love and respect. Just remember the longer it takes you to acquire this lesson, the more prolonged it will take good to be returned to you. There is a process of solving every problem going on in your life. So, stop expressing discontent and find yours. When you make the choice to change from the inside, your life will noticeably change on the outside. Others will respond to how you deal with them and deserve to be dealt with respect until they proved they do not show the qualities worthy of any form of admiration. Learn to ignore situations that may prove harmful to you. Reacting to anger can be irreversible and catastrophic, causing you more mental anguish than those you intended to hurt. Life is precious, so spend as much time as possible with those you love. You are not promised tomorrow. TYJ

July 15

Are you part of the problem or part of the solution? When you are a part of the problem, you take no responsibility for your actions. It is always someone else's fault that you reacted the way you did. You have no concept of the fact that you choose to react the way you did. Your childish self-centered reaction is a way of life. When you are a part of the solution, you take responsibility for your actions. You see your part in any situation. You apologize for your behavior and vow to do better next time. You love acting like a mature adult and wonder why it took so long to get there. There will be days when you question if you can continue. You become insecure and feel like you are falling apart. Remember, after all you are human. It is your choice, inner peace or turmoil. Learn your lessons and move on but never give up. With morning prayer and meditation, you can grow into maturity. Each day you will be inspired to become a better person. With God's guidance, you become excited to be alive. You learn to stay away from negative people and look for things that challenge you. You are grateful for your new way of life and no longer seek situations that clutter your mind with undesirable thoughts. What used to be your confused situation is now your moral work of art. TYJ

July 16

Your mirror can serve 2 purposes. 1st you are looking at the problem for if you are not the problem there is no solution. With morning prayer and meditation, God will help to heal your pains of past experiences thus giving you hope for the future. Show God your courage by surrendering to his will. Know that with God's guidance you will find the strength to face your tomorrows with confidence and strength knowing you will make it. Your goal will be to show kindness to others without seeking reward. Once you have learned these lessons, the person you are looking at in the mirror will be a kind, wholesome, loving person who is showing the maturity of walking away from people who threaten your serenity and feelings of self-worth. 2nd, it is a great place to put your positive affirmation notes to read while putting on makeup or shaving. Be grateful for the people God sent to help you on your journey of recovery. TYJ

July 17

Do not let fear, unkind people or insecurities ruin your day for old behavior may overtake what you have worked so hard to obtain. Stay in the present with morning prayer and meditation while creating positive thoughts. Sometimes things will need to go bad before they can get better. Karma must be dealt with because of bad choices already made. People will come and go in your life. Work on becoming the person God has prepared you to be. Occasionally you must be broken to find out how strong you really are. Remember the times you thought you were not going to make it? But here you are, alive and vibrant. You will handle and survive anything coming your way. The blessings you receive will be far greater than the burdens you encounter. With God's guidance, you will change the dynamics of what others think of you. Be grateful for all the times God has protected you. Now go out and do good for others. Before you leave the house, do not forget to blow a kiss to the lovely person in the mirror. TYJ

July 18

Know that you can learn something from everyone. All you really need is a few heroes to show you how beautiful life can be when you make the choice to save yourself from destruction. They start with helping you to feel good about yourself. They constantly remind you that you are worthy of God's love. You may make them mad, or you may become angry and frustrated with them, but they choose to stand with you in your time of need. A byproduct of finding out who you really are is you will make the choice to enhance your quality of life by grasping the skills needed to accept your flaws. True happiness starts with you. Once you can tolerate yourself, you will be free to find someone to add to your life. Do not let your bad choices define who you are. When the time is right for you, you will make the choice to modify your behavior but not 1 second before you are ready. You have experienced feelings of sadness, but you never gave up. Many blessings and healthier times were the result of your toughness. You have digested the skills of who you want to be and with God's guidance, you can become the new you without worrying about what others think. You were not created to please everyone. Just God. Remember it is in the seeking. Master the knowledge needed to enjoy today. TYJ

July 19

Special people enter your life for a reason, a season or a lifetime. Know their purpose and why you are involved with them for they are God sent. They do small things for you. Give you a favorite coffee mug. You read a book they recommend. You have car trouble, or a lawnmower does not work, and they fix it. These people are full of love and kindness. There are others who are sent to teach you lessons you refuse to learn. You keep making the same mistake no matter how many times someone has been sent to help you. It may start out as a gentle message at work or on TV. You can read it or hear it repeatedly and nothing sinks in. then one day it will make sense and you make the change. I can just hear God saying, "Well that took long enough." Be grateful for the a-holes that are sent to you. Learn your lesson and move on. There will be people who no matter how nice you are to them they will treat you badly. They will not value your kindness and trust. Look to God for your favorable life. When you can see the good in yourself you will be able to see it in others. Look for love and honesty. Fill your heart with gratitude. Learn to let go and you will enjoy the ride for not everyone is going to appreciate you. Maintain your dignity by removing yourself from the situation for you have learned a valuable lesson for the next time. TYJ

July 20

Look for people who have your best interests in mind and are not watching out for their own agenda. Using your instincts to guide you check out their motives and what they must gain. Look for people who want you as a friend and do not let them use you or try to control your feelings or emotions. Learn to keep past traumas from affecting today's decisions or let people convince you that your insights are just insecurities. Ever wonder why your life is so hard? It is the only way God can get your attention. Want a healthier life? Make sophisticated choices. Check where your intensity is for that is where your aspirations will be spent today. The more defeatist your concentration the more hardships you bring into your life. Make the choice to do right and happiness and self-love will be your reward. Go with your gut feelings for they come from the soul. Along with God's guidance, you will aspire to improve your style of life. Your voice of Love needs to be louder than the Darkness around you. Live each day with toughness and vitality drowning out any naysayer outlook of doom and gloom, along with your refusal to accept facts. TYJ

July 21

If you are that special person sent to help those psychologically different from the self, be grateful for God has blessed you with a mission and a purpose in life. Your good will always be returned in an extraordinary fashion. Be the one who helps for the betterment of society for people who give are always happier than the takers. I love your gift to humanity will be the one blessing you can take with you when you pass. Not one material thing will matter. Pray that the takers will finally find peace and tranquility. Once they make the choice to change, God will work quickly in their lives to help them find a true sense of belonging. Your happiness starts with you. Loneliness comes from not being pleased with your work on becoming a better person and your own selflove will be a byproduct. Once your actions improve, you will be able to make the choice to be happy. Until then, the Darkside will be your guide. Today's encounters will be tomorrow's power. Learn to live a life that matters being built on character, patience and love. TYJ

July 22

When you make false promises and do something different, don't be surprised if people pull away from you. Be a person of your word for that is the only thing you really have. Material things are possessions to help you with the impression that you are worth something. Your true happiness comes from the inside. Use morning prayer and meditation to help you when you don't agree with someone while remaining kind and loving to them. They are entitled to their opinion even if it doesn't make sense to you. Remember just because you think it does not mean it is right. Always say what you intended to but don't be cruel about it. You do not always have to figure everything out. Turn it over to God for He will give you your answer. Be cautious of anyone whose opening line is, "trust me." Put your reliance in God and what they say in context. Does it stand the test of love and kindness or fall into a category of gossip or self-gain? If you are offended, it may be because they are getting too close to old pains you may need to work on. Yes, always forgive every time. Placing care in them again is not always part of God's plan. Your knowledge will surprise you. TYJ

July 23

Special message just for today. In case you were wondering who must change in order to make you happy there is but one simple answer. It is never God, your father or mother, your brothers or sisters, your significant other or children who must change. The only person needed to change is you for only you can make you happy. Your dysfunction will remain if you blame others for your miserable life. Your insane disorder will cause you to act childlike with bouts of rage while suffering from severe depression. God has no problem using pain to get you to change. Rarely do people make the choice to change because they see errors in their ways. Bad situations that happen in life can be caused because of karma. You want good, then do good. Know what your passion in life is and choose to live in that manner. Learn to stop the negativity by taking the time to help others. TYJ

July 24

Your conceptions affect your life. So. may your day be filled with good, developed intentions; kind, loving people and happy occasions. Choose to be around people who value and cherish you because your happiness will depend upon it. For only you are responsible for your happiness. You are not capable of receiving more love than you have achieved in your own spiritual existence. This is not rocket science. You want more love? Work on becoming a better person so your love of self can improve. God has sent people to help you. It commences with a grateful heart so give attention to finding something in nature or a gift to give someone. The closer you are to the Darkside, the less willing you will be able to help others and are known as takers. Always believe in yourself and have faith in your potential. Walk away from people who threaten your morals and values. People with a strong sense of self-respect and a high degree of self-esteem tend to do what is right. Always seek God in times of uncertainty. Deceptive pride gets us away from following a good solid form of direction. Without God's guidance you can get into a misleading perception that you deserve all the credit for anything good going on in your life and none of the bad when your life hits rock bottom. I know you can only understand this according to your level of perception. The Darkside can only allow so much Truth to filter in at a time because He does not want to lose His followers. TYJ

July 25

If you wait for the perfect job, home or love life you may be waiting for a long time. You must do your homework while refraining from acting too quickly. There is a big difference between buying a pair of socks or a car. Choose wisely, learning to be happy with what you have while working on getting better and letting God reward you in His time. Do not make the same mistakes when God gives you new opportunities. Soft and gentle is the best while avoiding loud antagonistic people. Emotional healing is an important part of your spiritual journey. You may not have parted on the best of terms with all the people who left you when their time had ended. Forgive and pray for them to find what they are looking for. Enjoy your time while growing from any experiences that were not the best. With morning prayer and meditation, make the choice to remove any defeatist naysayers from your life when possible. Do not ignore or overlook defects for everyone has imperfections for that is their identity. Are their constructive attributes beneficial to outweigh their unfavorable qualities substantially enough to keep them as friends or more importantly as a significant other? Your choice. TYJ

July 26

By my choices I have caused my life to be good or bad. Today with God's guidance, I will make better choices so that at the end of the day I can say I did the best that I could. I have not rationalized or justified my insane behavior. I have not tried to control anyone or any situation. I did not get stressed over others not doing what I wanted them to do. I cannot change any past behavior, but I can make amends. With help from my spiritual advisor, I can ensure that I will not make those bad choices again. I will do my best to show people my heart has taken on a new kindness. I will have fun, be soft and gentle by being always myself while bringing joy and love to the world. I will set new goals without letting any of my past problems get in the way. I may fail and make mistakes; my heart may be broken for I am not perfect. I rise, I learn, I am alive, and I am grateful. Not everyone will like me. I will spend my time with people who appreciate me. People who make the choice to turn their back on me no matter how good I am to them may leave me with feelings of abandonment. I must realize there is nothing I can do about the situation. My mind needs quiet time in the morning to reflect on my purpose for that day. I take the time to put my calendar in order. I may not get everything done today. I will train my mind to be okay with that. The stress and anxiety caused from feelings of failure are not good for my wellbeing. After doing the best that I can for today I will give the outcome to God. Things are not always going to go my way. I need to be okay with that. My singleness of purpose is to help others. I do not allow past failures to bring about anger, regret or sadness. TYJ

July 27

With God's guidance and an honest look at your defects, you will become a better person than you were yesterday. It is imperative that you get up one more time than you have fallen. The most difficult part will be when you come to the realization that you may not be as important to some people as you thought you were. Your growth will show on how you handle this. It is not about how important you think you are. It is about being a realist, having humility, being forgiving to all and showing love and kindness when helping mankind. Will you have enough self-love and feelings of self-worth to be strong enough to survive without the use of other substances? Only by facing real life situations and asking for God's help will you know that answer to that. Or will you revert to old behavior from the Darkside and react with fearful, damaged, bewildered, emotional obsessive anger? Your choice. Please put your trust in God to help you make the choice to act as an adult. TYJ

July 28

Today I am striving for honesty, directness and clarity. I have gained an insight that I am required to listen to my soft gentle voice which generates from my soul. I know that true happiness is a personal thing and has nothing to do with anyone else. I have discovered the only thing I can control is how I react to situations. Will I proceed with peace and serenity or fear and anger? I pray I choose wisely. My actions are required to match my principles, so I do not have an obligation to rationalize and justify my behavior. I will live within the confines of my vision for today. I am thankful for everything in my Universe for I know that happiest person in the room leads the simplest life. Not reacting because of my fear of failure is in fact a failure. A simple lesson bestowed upon me was to let go of what is essential and face whatever comes my way with God's guidance for I am a powerful, distinctive, exonerating, guarded child of God. I have gained strength and sensitivity along with being a kind, loving person. Just don't push me too far for I do have limits and will not be used. TYJ

July 29

I may fail and make mistakes. My heart may be broken. I am not perfect. I rise, I learn, and I am alive and grateful. Not everyone will like me. I do not waste time on people who do not see my value. I spend my time with people who appreciate me. I walk away from anyone or anything that is venomous to my soul. People who make the choice to turn their back on me no matter how good I am to them may leave me with feelings of abandonment. I must realize there is nothing I can do except to accept the situation. My mind requires quiet time in the morning to reflect on my purpose for that day. I take the time to put my calendar in order. I am aware of the possibility of me not getting everything done today. I will train my mind to be okay with that. The stress and anxiety caused from feelings of failure are not beneficial to my wellbeing. After doing the best that I can for today I will give the outcome to God. Not every situation is always going to go my way. I feel an obligation to be okay with that. TYJ

July 30

Find out what you want out of life and with the guidance of your Higher Power allow it to happen. Acquire the skills to grow where your feet are planted. Just for today, make the choice to enjoy a condition or situation. If you so desire, you can choose to be miserable. Either one will work for both are correct according to how you are reacting to any given situation. Please make the choice to face your demons so peace and serenity can enter your life. Your being hurt must stop. If you allow the problem to exist, you have given your approval or authorization to remain unchanged. Your goal for today is to find a purpose in life. You are a worthy person deserving of a happy life. You will be careful as to who you let into your heart and will always react on the side of caution knowing your Guardian Angel will walk through hell with you to keep you moving forward. On the positive side, the more pain you have endured the greater will be your empathy for others. TYJ

July 31

Do not look at your life as a failure. See it as of all the ways you have tried nothing has worked so far. The world has enough haters and critics. Encourage others to fill their existence with love and kindness and that you are about to change and grow. Spend your quiet time in the morning listening to the soft gentle voice to find God's purpose for you. It is never the same for everyone while on the other hand, God's will for everyone is always to forgive no matter what the offense might have been. Hold no resentments, always help others while treating them with dignity and respect. Your parents may not have taught you the finer characteristics of happiness. It is never too late to acquire the skills needed to lead a spiritual existence by being a friend to the lonely. Always look for the good in yourself and others. Repeat your spiritual trip towards a greater understanding of your trust in God, to others. Help them to overcome the Darkside. Show them that their survival is truly a beautiful excursion and that they too can triumph over their past transgressions. Be an inspiration to others to seek a God of their understanding. Let them know that God sees no value in sadness. Satan can only offer you stuff. It is God who will help you to heal from the inside where all the deep pain that the Darkside has caused is stored waiting for you to expand your vision of what a beautiful tale and achievement your healing will be. Rocket science is not practiced here. All you need to do is make the choice with God's assistance to change. TYJ

August 1

People who are uplifting are a treasure. They share their unselfishness with everyone. For those who are not, the higher my degree of self-worth, the better equipped I am to handle them. The more they whine, the stronger the chance they will attract things to be dissatisfied with. Their internal upheaval is caused by being controlled by the Darkside and has nothing to do with you. I often turn to the help of my Angels to cope with difficult people. I am filled with gratitude for the person I am today, and I thank that individual who I was 44 yrs. ago for not giving up the fight to survive. My mind can only handle one concept at a time so I think positive thoughts so negativity will be blocked out. With morning prayer and meditation, I can start my day being delivered from past failures along with the freedom of selfish behavior belonging to fear and anxiety. I am continually expanding my wisdom while on my journey of recovery, gaining dignity and filling my soul with God's love. The first occurrence of discouragement, I start praying. I would never knowingly let a thief in my house to steal my God given possessions so why would I start my day with any discouraging thoughts. Today I am led by experience and dignity, not fear for I am victorious over my past adverse lifestyle. TYJ

August 2

If you wish to love in a world without fear, anxiety or anger issues; stop creating them. With morning prayer and meditation, start with positive thoughts and at any time during the day when a negative thought or fear starts to overtake you, stop and ask God to remove them. Negative people thrive on drama, fear and anxiety. My life may not be a bowl of cherries, but it does not mean I have to eat the pits. Life can be happy if you stay positive, count your blessings, and strive for humility while learning from your mistakes. A simple smile will better your mood by relieving stress. Happiness is an inside job. Do not look for someone who makes you happy. Strive to find a special person who adds to your happiness. In the meantime, work on yourself to become a better person so when the right person does come along, they do not reject you because you are a selfish, self-centered, angry nutcase. Putting God 1st, others 2nd and yourself 3rd does not mean you do not take care of yourself. Rest when you are tired. Eat when hungry. Take time to talk to your spiritual advisor when you feel lonely and always work on your anger issues. You can't give away what you do not have. Your own happiness will depend upon how you view your Universe. TYJ

August 3

With morning prayer and meditation, seek God's guidance and bring outstanding karma into your existence. This means you react to life with a kind, loving, giving, compassionate, grateful, forgiving, generous nature. Being under the Darkside's guidance brings adverse karma to yourself. One characteristic will be you acting as a selfish self-centered a-hole. Your choice, either way works. Your happiness depends upon your attitude. Negativity causes a lot of people's lonely, sad existence. Self-doubt can cause a lack of self-judgment. We strive to want people to like and accept us. You do what it takes to be loved thus affecting your moral values. Hang with people who are God-centered for they will help you with your low self-esteem by encouraging you to do right. Trust your instincts because your gut feelings are insights from your Angels. Thinking what you do on all occasions, failing all else, will give you what you continually got. TYJ

August 4

Do not let people who doubt you or try to limit your ability to do an overview of your being a vital and functioning human affect you. Your life has gone from hoping that morning prayer and meditation will work to faith that it does work. Focus on the lesson not the pain. Find out what triggers your negative reactions. You used to worry about people who did not like you until you learned that most people have problems liking themselves. Haters are going to dislike you. Just make sure you are not one of them. Your life has been a total turnaround from the time you suffered from fear, anxiety and rage. You find that every single problem can be solved if you take the time to contemplate God's direction and put things into a simple interpretation. You no longer chase after the things you feel you needed. You have gained the patience and wisdom from that pain to allow God to bring them to you if He desired that you have them. You are grateful that God pulled you from that pit of Darkness and gave you a new life. Listen for the enlightenment of the soft gentle voice from within. TYJ

August 5

Find your level of peace by continuing to forgive, trust and love. Positive thoughts take up just as much space as the negative ones that you allow to control your mind. Free yourself from the confinement of your own erroneous conceptions. The more you walk away from the components that are infectious to your immortal being, the more pleasurable your life will be. To love yourself means that you accept the person you are. God has loved you through the worst of times so care enough about yourself to fight for a better life. Through morning prayer and meditation and a nightly inventory you can continue to let go of the anger and bitterness while growing in kindness, peace of mind and love. Allow the light to shine through your Darkness. It is time to stop taking everyone else's account of their daily transgressions and start viewing your own for if you are not the problem there is no solution. The most contented people are the ones taking a recap of their own shortcomings, not judging others. TYJ

August 6

Be gentle, kind and loving for if you do not find peace from within you will never find it anywhere else. People may annoy, anger or cause you to be fearful. Learn your lesson, for they are there to teach you patience, forgiveness and courage. Gain knowledge in your ability to let go of any situation you have no control over by trusting the Universe. Do not judge others by your story for they have their own narrative to tell. It is not a good idea to compel others to be in your life. Instead, appreciate the people that God puts in your existence. You have gone through a lot to get to where you are today. Be grateful for your story and tell it when asked for you may be the one God sent to help someone to survive. Enjoy the company of others, the love and kindness that they show for that is what life is all about. Material things are nice, but this is not why you wake up every day. You did your inventory last night and found out you could have been more generous and caring to the people you encountered. So today when doing your morning prayer and meditation, confirm that you are going to exceed in being compassionate and affectionate to the people you meet today. TYJ

August 7

Open your heart to the world around you. You came into your newfound spirituality as a rosebud all closed with self-centeredness. With morning prayer and meditation, you have opened as a rose in all its glory. You recognize the full implications of every single human being who makes the choice to change their existence to brighten up your day. You naturally gravitate towards people who appreciate you. God gives you the free will to turn back into an a-hole at any time you choose. Your inventory last night showed that you can still do a better job of being warmhearted and caring. How will you know when you are generous enough? The Pope will send you a notification that you are being recognized as a Saint. Letting your Ego get in the way by showing anger to one person nullifies all your acts of kindness for that day. Making amends for that act of selfish self-centeredness puts you back in good standing with the Universe. TYJ

August 8

God will send people to help you gain the knowledge to absorb your lessons, but the tasks are still yours to experience. Mostly the instructions will be painful for it appears you do not listen to the soft gentle voice when things are going great. So, absorb your tutoring quickly and get on with getting better while maintaining a grateful attitude. Remember it was through morning prayer and meditation you asked for God's guidance to help you become a better person so you can live a life without bitterness, hurt, anxiety and depression. Look for circumstances you do not like about yourself and pray for the courage to change. Your growth may be painful but staying stuck in your old ways is not an option you can choose to continue to live with so God will no longer have to send negativity into your life. Today, true friends come into your existence to share your happiness, prosperity and tranquility. Peace and serenity can be yours for the taking. May your spiritual growth be a contagious feeling of clarity and awareness so one you are restored to love and kindness, you can choose to help others mend. TYJ

August 9

Today you have a new opportunity to become a better person. Not everything in your life is going to be a lesson or a result of bad karma. Some tasks will be a blessing because of the good you have done for others. Be grateful for both and allow solutions to enter your mind. Put your trust in God for He is forging you into the person He always meant you to be. You are enough. Know the enemy for He will plant seeds of disapproval in your thinking like God doesn't care for you. You are evil and not worthy of having qualities required for a particular role. By starting your day with morning prayer and meditation, your Darkside will lose his influence over you. Do not under any circumstances seek revenge for those who have harmed you. Be smart and let God handle what is due to them. Not everyone will see your worth and that's okay just if it is not you. Let God direct your steps for His Karma will be on time. Choose who you want to be around so peace and quietness can fill your life. You are not responsible for people who follow their own erroneous ideas of who they think you are. Their rudeness reveals who they are, and their lies show they do not consider your abilities to see the truth. They think you are too ignorant to know the distinction of their perceptions. TYJ

August 10

Live your life without stress or worries by not allowing your negative reasoning to steal your happiness. The quiet solitude of the morning is the best time to put your concentration in order starting with being grateful for what you have and by solving your problems with rational reasoning. You may feel different or that you do not fit in. God has a special purpose for you. Through morning prayer and meditation, seek God's guidance to find out what your role is by putting your exploits in a positive point of view thereby stopping your compulsive negative thinking. Not everyone you meet today is going to treat you with love and kindness. You may not be afforded the opportunity to distance yourself or close family members from rage or negativity. Use prayer to react to their outrage. Not all people are God-centered. Do not allow yourself to be one of them. The Darkside has His army, and it is important to know the Enemy. In real wars, the ones with the best and most guns win. In God's wars, the ones with the greatest and ultimate prayers win. When being faced with rage, do not react with anger. Keep asking God to bless the person until the Enemy can be neutralized and peace restored. TYJ

August 11

Forget the bad choices you made in the past. Your Higher Power has dropped the charges so now it is time for you to find tranquility by forgiving yourself and others. What was meant to destroy you never touched your soul. Money may be tight right now. It cannot buy honesty, acceptance, love, kindness or peace. Concentrate on your choices today. With morning prayer and meditation, you can stop the chaos by choosing to participate in your own recovery thus achieving your objective of becoming a better person. You will need to do more than think about improving. You will have to put in the effort needed to realize your ambitions. Be around people who make you laugh so they can help to improve your quality of accomplishments. Seek God's guidance in all your affairs today. Do all your tasks with a good heart without prejudice or judging others harshly. Use unconditional love instead. If you are tired of feeling like shit, make the choice to stop living in your cesspool commonly known as the Darkside. TYJ

August 12

By following God's guidance and starting your morning with prayer and meditation, you allow God to help you to live a life of increased wellness. Therefore, a special spiritual development can be obtained. You are better able to handle stress, anger and sadness. You will express your emotions in a healthy manner and obtain a higher level of self-esteem. Tonight, when reviewing your day pay close attention to how many times you complained about how displeasing your day was. Do you want to stop having lame days? Stop thinking about how uncool your day was because by thinking negatively you attract a defeated attitude into your life. This is not rocket science. Stop complaining and think happy thoughts and that is what you will attract into your life. Smile, don't worry, expect a little, give a lot, stay in the here and now and being grateful are all keys to happiness. TYJ

August 13

Live life without fear or anxiety. Breathe God in and fear out. Breathe God in and anxiety out. By asking God to join you in your day you will be able to focus on the positive. Know that the actions of others have nothing to do about you and says everything about them. They will find offense with everything you do. Wish only good for them and positive karma will come back to you. Each day is a new beginning, and you get to choose how you will respond to it. Please make the choice to bring cheer into your life. Only you can create your thoughts which generates your feelings and they in turn cause your actions. You must exist in these 24 hours. You can spend it living with either joy or hostility. Your choice. Do not continue to blame past circumstances for your nasty behavior. Treat each difficult situation or condition connected with or relevant to an event or negative action as a lesson for learning. Not as, why does stuff keep happening to me? There is nothing you can do to stop bad karma from catching up to you because of past bad choices. Forgive those who have harmed you. Prayer is an excellent healer. Do it for them and your peace of mind. TYJ

August 14

View fear as "False Evidence Appearing Real" and worry as soul suicide. Stop the drama of toxic friends and bad self-degrading analysis. Take time each day to give yourself a "well done" by striving for excellence, not perfection. Telling yourself good thoughts so God can keep sending you miracles. You are worthy, special, talented and a unique person. God made only one of you and He does not make junk so please do not wish to be anyone else. Your mind can either be a faithful companion or a hostile adversary. By starting your day with morning prayer and meditation you will do all the good you can. At the end of the day thank God for helping you make it through another 24 hours showing gratitude for the day you have just accomplished by acknowledging the kindness and compassion you showed others. Bad times are temporary once you put good karma into motion, God's blessings last forever. Staying calm through all your current circumstances gives you the opportunity to seek God's guidance thus supporting you to gain trust in your Higher Power while encouraging you to refrain from overthinking or overreacting. TYJ

August 15

Living in the past is playing into your Darkside's web. You play the self-imposed downer game of "what if or if only this had happened." Suppose you have someone who is driving you crazy. You ask God for the power to change how you deal with them otherwise the Enemy uses these opportunities to fill you with shame and regret. When living in the future, your lower power will fill you with fear and anxiety. With morning prayer and meditation, you can get aligned with your Universe thus helping you to get your mind where your feet are which for all practical purposes should be inside your hula hoop. You learn to trust your feelings not your thinking. You do not wait to see what kind of day you are going to have. You make it your choice to live in today by planning to have a great day filled with positive thoughts of serenity, calm and happiness. TYJ

August 16

You need to let go of what you thought should happen and accept what is happening as God's will for you, learning to swim with the tide rather than against it. If you have been badly hurt in a relationship it may take more time for the heart to trust what the mind already knows. With morning prayer and meditation, you can start your day with a positive attitude looking at each day with a blank page that you can rewrite your life with. Your choice. Stay in the shitty or start your day with a new shiny outlook on life. I was asked by an extremely negative narcissistic person what I got out of all this prayer and meditation stuff. I had to stop and think about that and then God sent me the answer. It isn't what I have gained. It is what I have lost which is an extremely negative life filled with rage and depression and I no longer must be right at all costs along with giving you permission to be wrong without contradicting or as my spiritual advisor would say, "let them suffer." I no longer hold back on the Truth so others can feel comfortable while living in the Darkside. TYJ

August 17

Do not let your Darkside trick you into believing that your happiness comes from living in the proper part of the city, driving the perfect car or dating that gorgeous babe or hunk. It is nice that your children got into the right school to get a solid education. Your real success story will be, did you teach them to be respectful and kind to others? There are benefits that come from putting your trust in God 1st and then reaping the rewards of His love for you. You receive your strength and protection from Him. He is your shield and will keep you in that place of safety. Do not let judging others take the place of right thinking. You cannot continue to sit on your couch hoping positive changes will take place in your life. After finishing your morning prayer and meditation, go out into the world and do something decisive and challenging. So what if you fail? It will keep you humble. God will keep you going, and your trials will keep you strong. God feels your pain and tears and has more blessings for you. You must quit living in the past and stop overthinking the "what ifs". Never fear change and remember you are enough. Your part is to never give up. TYJ

August 18

Happiness comes to those who appreciate what they have for life does not have to be perfect to be admired. Cherish your life for it is too short not to enjoy it. Get rid of anger and fear with morning prayer and meditation. Put your fears and worries of the future on paper and ask God to remove them for tomorrow is not yet here. Make solid choices and then turn them over to God. Yesterday is gone and cannot be changed. If you hurt someone, make amends. If you stole something, make restitution. Create a daily choice, an appropriate moment not to go back to the person you were by viewing each day as a new beginning. You may have scars from your childhood that have taken a long time to heal. Prayer and forgiveness go a long way in helping you to trust God's timing for He will make a way for you. TYJ

August 19

Be satisfied knowing that today will be better than yesterday because you started your day with morning prayer and meditation. You create a joyful life by being grateful for the difficult people in your life. They made you the strong person you are today. Just for today, compliment someone by telling them how much you admire them and how great it is to have them as a friend. You will both feel better about yourselves. Giving to others is great if you don't burn yourself out. Take the time to rest when needed. Your past may not have been the best. Make the choice to change your future to amazing. It starts with becoming aware of who is good for you and who is not. Do not allow negativity, president criticism or insults to affect your life. Choose to walk away from the toxic people that you can. Those you cannot, start with praying for them to want to alter their lives. Your transformation will begin when you make the choice to give attention to your inside wickedness. TYJ

August 20

Gods will for you is to seek harmony, freedom and health. In your morning prayer and meditation, ask God to bless your body and claim perfect wellness. Take the time to learn natural medicine, for drugs are meant to stop the pain and herbal medicines heal the body. Excellent health comes from calmness of mind. You are substantially capable of handling your most prominent weakness. By your actions, you will take the 1st step to victory. Choose to let what happens to you make you better not bitter. Smoldering resentments, rage and anger lead you to becoming a victim of yourself. Living in the past may lead to depression. Worry and anxiety contribute to unsound health problems. Bring peace and serenity into your life. Start with a simple prayer of general amnesty by freely forgiving everyone who has ever harmed you in any fashion. TYJ

August 21

Laugh often for it is good for the soul and helps to make things less difficult and overwhelming. Through morning prayer and meditation, you learn to uplift the negative enslavement of your mind. Know your flaws and weaknesses for they give you the strength to learn from past mistakes. Have the faith to stay on course and know that God will supply what is best for you because past actions can cause long-term consequences. Your biggest problem is having a non-forgiving personality therefore no matter what good comes your way you will never be happy. Don't let past damages ruin your life. Healing starts when you forgive. Spiritual growth is a byproduct of letting go. May you start your road to recovery today. Be forgiving and watch your life blossom with abundant grace and harmony. It takes a lot of selflove to restore old wounds to wholeness and spirituality. When asking for the strength to endure, God will give you difficulties to build up your resistance to temptation for God is preparing you for your chosen purpose. TYJ

August 22

You gain strength by accepting your weaknesses and favorable experiences when you learn from them. When you blame others for your troubles you believe that your situation must come from out there. If you acquire nothing else, gain the knowledge that you solve your difficulties from within. You ask God to remove your faults and work on growing. With the beauty of morning prayer and meditation, you can start each day as a new page in your life. One nice thing about finding out who you really are is that you can also determine who you want to become. You have the power to create that person for God is all powerful. You acquire a unique ability to touch other's lives with your story. You did not go through all this crap just to keep it to yourself. Let go of cynicism, fear and anxiety. Focus on a favorable outcome or lesson on all your life situations of deterioration. You can either keep living in adversity or change. Your choice. Just for today, freely forgive everyone and start your journey of becoming a useful person in society. TYJ

August 23

You do not have to be alone anymore. Let the Grace of God enter your life with morning prayer and meditation. By seeking His guidance, you get rid of your ego, false pride and ignorance. They have ruined enough of your romantic endeavors. You will then find peace, and everything will fall into place. A toxic involvement is being with a controlling insecure dominant self-centered person. Fears are learned from childhood. You may have forgotten the incident, but the unease is lodged into your subconscious. Do not let those doubts consume your intelligence or judgment. Ask God to remove your fears. It is okay to have struggles in your life. God allows them so you can learn to reach out to Him. Your part is to ask for help. Since God has got this, choose to reach out with positive thoughts. He will make a way for you by giving you courage to overcome any situation. Thus, putting your mind at ease with peace and tranquility. You must remain fearless, not letting anxiety overtake your thoughts. By staying positive you are on your journey to finding God's purpose for you. Just for today, forgive everyone. TYJ

August 24

Just in case you had no idea, you are special and worthy of love. Say what you mean but do not say it cruelly. God sees each of you has unique and forgives you for your flaws. He does not want you buying into drama or negativity. Be grateful for both your sad and happy times. One teaches you lessons while the other brings you joy. Stay positive no matter how hopeless your situation may appear. You are lovable. Listen to the soft gentle voices of your angels. Do not put yourself down. Be kind to oneself. Practice letting go of what you cannot control. Do not do for others so they will like you. Do for them with kindness and love. Those who say it cost nothing to be kind have never met a narcissist. Be careful out there. Never settle for being 2nd best in yours or someone else's life. Make the choice to be always #1. You cannot love others more than you love yourself. Only you are responsible for any choices you make so it is time to stop blaming others. Always keep your emotions intact. Be grateful when God redirects your prayers to something better. TYJ

August 25

Leave the tension, worry and pain behind. Choose to live a joyous, happy and peaceful life. While living in the presence of God with morning prayer and meditation, think positive words of success, healing and joy. Sometimes you just need someone to listen without interrupting. You do not always need worldly advice. You may just need to get released from guilt or shame feelings of people who have neglected or harmed you. The most unselfish thing we can do to relieve our pain is to help others who are suffering their own hidden fears and anxieties. You need to let them do what they need to do to make themselves peaceful. It is okay to give advice when asked and then mind your own business for each person must walk their own trail. Do check up on them from time to time. You may think they are taking too long. It is their path, and they can walk it at their speed. Let it go and let God handle them. TYJ

August 26

Your life is forever changing. What you feel today, this month or this year will not last forever. You need to consider your feelings without dwelling on the negative aspects of them. Your spiritual journey doesn't begin until you reach your emotional bottom. God wants you to learn from your mistakes for the pain and suffering will continue until you do. Your actions need to align with your principles and morals so you can stop rationalizing and justifying your behavior. It is essential that you start your day with morning prayer and meditation and bring God into your life. Does your close circle of friends bring joy into your life along with motivating and inspiring you? Two things can be happening here. Either you need to get a better class of friends, or you can choose to work on changing your life for the better. You make the choice on how you react to life situations. The more difficult your existence the bigger God's plan for you. Forgive everyone who has ever harmed you. TYJ

August 27

Do not settle for someone who is willing to give you all the worldly goods. Find someone who is eager to give you their time, attention and constant love. You were not perfect. Your scars will heal. Let go of the past. Keep any expectations real. Pay attention to people's tactics so you will not be fooled by their words. A promise is only a manipulation unless followed by a positive performance. A toxic person will use devious emotional exportations. Learn to recognize the difference between poor social habits and an unscrupulous personality. Without respect and honesty, love is unstable. It needs to be felt from the heart, not just given lip service. You are worthy of true love. People grow mentally and spiritually when loved properly. When God sends you troubled people to help, always start with loving them unconditionally. Be careful not to let their Darkness harden your soul. You may not be able to go back and fix all your mistakes. You will be qualified to help others see theirs. Always be a forgiving person. TYJ

August 28

Too much worry steals today's happiness. The pieces will fall into place so until then laugh at the confusion because everything happens for a reason. Remember, God has got this. Only Light can drive out Darkness and love the world's hatred. Your mind believes what you think. Tell it you are healing, not broken. Problem free, not filled with negativity. Your pains will one day be your strengths. May you prepare for a joyous life by starting with loving your neighbor and yourself. What irritates you about your mate or friends is usually your starting point when looking at yourself. Notice how selfish people are. It took years to see how selfish and self-centered I really was and how everything was about me. With morning prayer and meditation, you will be able to overcome all your spiritual maladies. Everyday ask God to help you to see the value in helping others. God blesses and protects everyone who honestly seeks Him. He will heal your hurts and relieve you of your pains. Your spiritual journey will set you free. TYJ

August 29

It may not always seem so, but you are okay, and everything will work out. You are given a chance to start your life over. Decide to make this one a masterpiece. Be positive, have faith that with God's guidance, all will be well. Be patient, endure any hardships. Continue to seek God's will and receive all He has promised you. Select an environment that will help bring you closer to your Maker. Appreciate all that you have, and your life will feel spectacular. The quicker you can quiet that loud chatty monkey voice in your mind, the faster your soul can heal your spiritual deformities. Pay attention to how you react to others or any life event. Why did this situation cause you to lose your temper? Your spiritual being is sending you a message. Something from your childhood is out of balance. Journal these reactions to your buttons being pushed. What fear has been reopened? Life is not about being perfect. It is about being kind to everyone. Forgive those who have harmed you. TYJ

August 30

Do not look for someone to help you feel better about yourself. 1st, fall in love with yourself and then share that love with someone who appreciates you. In morning prayer and meditation, tell God your needs and thank Him for all He has done for you. Do everything quietly with a calm heart. Anytime your spiritual calmness is threatened, stop what you are doing and ask God to remove your fears and anxieties. When your inner peace is restored, resume your day. With all the time you spend thinking to yourself maybe you need to make kinder references to your ability to handle life situations. When ceasing to feel a resentment against another, you do not have to face the person or let them know you are letting go of a grudge towards them. You are exonerating them for what they did to you either real or imagined. It has nothing to do with how they feel towards you. It is none of your business what they think of you. It is for your peace of mind, not theirs. TYJ

August 31

Appreciate everything that goes on in your life today. A good day will give you happiness. A bad day will give you experience. Your worst day will give you a lesson and prepare you for what you have been asking for. Be strong, courageous and a person of your word. You are not perfect. You will make erroneous statements or do harm to others. They have the right to be displeased with your actions. Make your amends and move on thanking God for giving you another chance to do right. It is by your actions that people will learn to respect you. Days are better when you start your morning with prayer and meditation, talking to God to find out his will for you. How you start your morning will create a positive outlook for the rest of the day. Think happiness for it is a spiritual experience of loving others. Listen to the soft gentle voice from within. At no time should you think of harming others. TYJ

September 1

Never allow someone else's love to dictate who they want you to be. Stay true to yourself and be who God created you to be. If God gives you the opportunity to change your life make the choice to do so. Life goes on whether you do it or not. You will never again wake up with regrets. Supportive intelligent thoughts will create a positive life. You may think that you can do nothing about others upsetting you for it is your fate in life. If you think it, you can unthink it. Your life shows either strengths or weaknesses. Pay close attention on how you react to any problem. Do you make excuses by rationalizing and justifying your actions or do you find solutions? Be cautious of anyone who finds a problem for every solution. Make the choice to walk with God for He will calm your mind and clear a path of self-love and kindness. When you pass you want one of your greatest achievements to be that you forgave others. TYJ

September 2

Align your thoughts with your heart and your actions with your words and you will have integrity when leading others to the Truth. God's will for you today is to have a humble heart when helping others to find love and kindness. Whenever you get in the mindset of judging others you need to remember that you also had a past. What will help you change your former self was to see what you really gained by changing your negative behavior. When you stop running away from your Darkside you will find a bright future. What others thought of you no longer was a big concern of yours and you started looking at how you saw yourself. Your spiritual journey starts with your thoughts. It cannot remain a mental transition forever. At some point on your road to a happy destiny. The truth will be your best offense. TYJ

September 3

You will meet people whose life is one big emotional series of events or tragedies. You do not have to attend the performance. You will go through periods of ups and downs. Don't get too high during the good times or wallow in self-pity during the low times. Let your pain heal. Learn your lesson while getting strength through the bad times and move on. When you hang on to things from the past you delay what God wants to bless you with today. By forgiving past injustices you will help change your future. Relax, let go and let God and things will work out when you let life happen. There are times you will not get what you want because God may be protecting you from a bad choice. With morning prayer and meditation, you can learn to take a stand. There will come a time in your life when enough is enough. You become willing to make a change for the better. Your purpose for today is to observe your reactions to the actions of others. Did you join in the drama? Have you learned to set healthy boundaries? It is okay to be yourself. May you make that choice starting today. TYJ

September 4

Do not lose sleep over things you cannot control. Always be who God intended you to be. Not everyone is going to like you. There will be close-minded people who blame you for everything going on in their lives. They see themselves as the important one and you are not. They cannot comprehend that you may have feelings also. Do not get discouraged or frustrated. Do not let them drag you down to their level. They do not have to like you just as importantly you do not have to waste your time caring. Spend your time looking at your own negative traits and karma will take care of them. Pay close attention to the healthy people you hang with. God will always send his angels to protect you. Pay close attention to your line of BS. Improve your message to include love and kindness. Work on replacing your EGO with self-respect. Choose only positive healthy thoughts to put into your spiritual being. TYJ

September 5

When the thought of being critical of another arises choose to ask God to bless them instead. Karma will have others blessing you rather than expressing adverse or disapproving judgments of you. Once you understand how the Universe works it will change your life. If you steal or lie, someone must return the favor. That works in every aspect of your life. Just because everyone else is doing it does not change universal laws. So, the choice is yours. Make it wisely. You may have practiced a negative lifestyle for so many years that it can take time for Karma to cause a change in your predicaments. With morning prayer and meditation, you can start a positive reaction to bring a new standard of happenings in your life. Start with sending love and kindness to all you meet today. This can be so foreign to you that you may have to start with an act as if policy. Your first thought does not have to be how you respond to any given situation. Take time to slow down your retaliation so you can counteract in a positive way. It will take time to alter or modify your thoughts. Embrace the new person you are becoming. Do not give up for your achievements will be worth the effort. True happiness will be your reward. TYJ

September 6

It is extremely difficult for the mind to maintain a positive attitude when as addicts we are always wanting more. We are an insufferable arrogant selfish lot consumed with resentments and rage. Along with a desire to spend wastefully to acquire more stuff or food to fill that empty hole in our soul. Known as gangrene of the soul. We should not be eager to praise ourselves for it is sweeter to let others give us approval. They will be closer to the truth for we have an exaggerated representation or ourselves. We need to learn to focus on things that matter. Trading limitation to operate within ourselves by concentrating on a nonmaterial purpose that brings us joy and happiness. With morning prayer and meditation, focus on things that you can control or change. This will help to bring less stress into your life. How can I tell when God is about to give me something special? The Darkside always comes at me harder with His lies and temptations to render me unfit to receive God's promises. Resentments are the Enemy's number one offender. When I do tonight's inventory on how I handled today I am going to thank God for being alive. Gratitude is the best antidote for keeping the Darkside at bay. Just be nice to someone today. It may find a warm spot in their heart for you. TYJ

September 7

When discussing a subject keep an open mind. Do not argue. You can disagree without being disagreeable. Having a mental connection with someone is rare so cherish it. You need to discuss your feelings of self-pity, shame, fear and anger. Work on your feelings of inadequacy and low self-esteem. Through morning prayer and meditation, you can realign yourself on how you respond to your emotions and adjust yourself to God's will. Practice leaving your comfort zone. It will help you to learn your abilities on how to get along with handling life on life's terms. Adjust to realities as you travel through your day. Quiet your fears by taking God with you. Choose to react with kindness and integrity. Never regret being kind to someone and giving them a selfish opportunity to use you for it says everything about them. For the less fortunate, a kind deed may make their day. At no time are you to think you are better than anyone else. TYJ

September 8

Be mindful of another's feelings. Your wit and humor may come across as sarcasm. Do not ignore your upset mental state. Stuffing your anxieties can cause resentments and depression. Excessive fear is a companion of false pride. It causes rage attacks, stomping away or striking back with cruel words. You tend to express your inadequate emotions by a change in your subconscious behavior giving you an aggravated perception of importance thus making up for your mental disturbance of feeling less than. Do random acts of kindness and love. Start with praying for others instead of gossiping about them. Get to know as many healthy people as you can. Watch how they react to others. Ask them about their view on subjects that you may be closeminded about. How have they learned to take the good with the bad? Is it impossible to think that every day is going to be a bed of roses? What is important is how you react when life gives you thorns. Ask how they have learned from their mistakes? If when asked through prayer, God does not change your situation, it may be for one of two reasons. You may not have learned your lesson, or you have not forgiven someone. Life will go on no matter how good or bad your attitude is. Happiness is a conscious effort to do right. God oversees your insides. The Darkside can only offer you stuff. May you choose constructive optimism. You are good enough. TYJ

September 9

Be interested in others. Let everyone you meet feel that you regard them as a person of importance. You may be the only person that helps them feel significant today. Choose to practice humility and perseverance to combat the actions of the Darkside. Start your morning with prayer and meditation to find out what God's strategy is for you today. Show determination in your willingness to help others. You have learned to take the good with the bad. There will be times during the day that you will need to readjust your focus on God's design for living. Never be so helpful that others can control you. Pay close attention to their motives. You can restart your day over as many times as needed. Do not get discouraged or unsure of yourself. God knows what you have need of. Trust Him for He will bring you through any adversity. No matter how bad your day is going always treat others with a loving heart. Just in case no one told you, you are a good lovable person. TYJ

September 10

As a grown up you need to stop blaming your loved ones for the way you turned out. Just because you have freedom of choice does not mean you are free from the consequences of your defeatist refusal to change. Be grateful for that part of your life. It gave you a better version of reality. People may not like your honesty. It interferes with their lies. Whether an optimist or a pessimist when your glass appears half full traded in for a smaller one. Be positive. No matter how hard your life was you can make the choice to find your own motivation to be free from addictions. It will be difficult to alter the direction your life is going. Things may get worse for a while. Self-sacrifice can leave you wanting. The one thing you have is that no one else is you. Your story is yours. Help others to find a mental stimulation to substitute their Darkside for a closer walk with God. He is better than anything you have going on in your life right now. TYJ

September 11

Take time to thank the people who helped to improve your life. Tell them how much you appreciate them. Live a life of gratitude so people do not have to walk on eggshells around you. All change starts on the inside with your thoughts. If at any time during the day something happens to cause you to become negative or your heart is bitter, be very cautious of what you say. Words can be very damaging. With morning prayer and meditation, seek God's guidance to get you back on track. There is never anything bad enough going on in your life to be disrespectful or downgrading to others. Restoring your hope and returning to your purpose in life is a powerful drug. Train your subconscious for that will be who you are tomorrow. When I surrender to God's will, He can do more for me then all the I wants that I may seek for myself. May we never forget. TYJ

September 12

Make promises sparingly but keep them faithfully at all costs. Obligations not kept are good intentions deemed not worthy of retaining. Thoughts of you bring back the implied hurt of the person on the other side of that agreement who felt slighted. A chain of events starts with a promise to do something for others. If you can't keep your word, a simple text or call will help to avoid frustration. Keep a list of your pending engagements so you can mark off the ones kept. If you were the one hurt by another's disregard for a promise made, do not stay angry or retaliate. Forgive them immediately and pray for them to become more understanding of another's feelings. Do not forget to list the promises made to yourself. They are: smile, sing, play, dream, pray and love yourself. Use the stuff you have bought and love the people God has sent to you. We do tend to switch those around. When the Darkside tells you that you are unworthy of anything good remind him that God loves you, sees you as exceptional and essential. Never seek the approval of others in order to validate yourself. TYJ

September 13

Discourage gossip for talking about another's vices is a major defect and can be destructive. Let your virtues speak for themselves. Through morning prayer and meditation, you will learn to be kind to others and yourself. Never accept less than you deserve you will have to go through whatever it takes to change your faults into moral principles. Why these lessons must destroy you first is beyond comprehension. Enlightenment will give you the opportunity to view them as they really are. Your life will be a lot less complicated. By acquiring the knowledge to love yourself you will consider yourself good enough to receive God's grace into your life. Do not let your EGO stand in the way of making amends. It will start with the willingness to become willing to agree to do them. No amount of begging, shaming or tough love is going to change a toxic person if they do not see any negativity in their life. Under no circumstances do you rationalize or justify their behavior. You on the other hand can be an example of God's love by never passing up an opportunity to do a kind deed for someone else. TYJ

September 14

I truly enjoy spending time with special friends along with quality time with myself. I do choose to withdraw from crowds when everyone is talking but do not have anything vital or refreshing to say. I act differently around fake people because I have a contrasting comfort zone around negative people. Choose your friends wisely, looking for people who appreciate, support and can help you with your misunderstandings about yourself. They will not let you get by with your BS. Your troubles will not last forever. It is okay to be sad. Just do not camp out there forever. People may treat you badly. It says more about them than you. Being rude is easier than doing the special work it takes to improve on your faults. God gives you permission to assume that everyone you meet today needs a kind word of encouragement. Always praise good work in public and when critiquing is needed do so behind closed doors. Gently, above all do not be arrogant. TYJ

September 15

Do not listen to despairing words others say about you. If you have a spiritual counselor, listen. They know your dark side. Who was there for you when you hit rock bottom? It does not hurt to go outside of your comfort zone occasionally. You are afforded the opportunity to either grow or run back and hide in your negativity. Master the knowledge on how to fight your Darkside. If God is working on removing your negativities do not question his motives. He will close doors when needed. Keep an open mind on morning prayer and meditation. You do not buy the 1st dress or suit that you try on. Keep experimenting until one feels right for you. You need to get rid of the bitterness of lost loves. Pray for positive energy and serenity when being alone. You do not need someone else to fill that empty hole. God is the answer. Silence your loud chattering monkey voice and let your soul heal itself. Not everyone will feel the need to change, and it is not your job to attempt to fix them. God will send a spiritual guide to give you clarity and wipe your tears while you are putting yourself back together. TYJ

September 16

Do not totally give up on a person changing. Pray for them to seek God's guidance and want to make the change. For some people, nothing you do is ever good enough. You cannot change anyone's thinking. In the meantime, choose to move on and stop watering a dead flower. You no longer waste time on nonsense. People come into your life to love and bless you and others test your patience. Either way they help to build character. It is important to know that not all spiritual advisors are of an earthly nature. Advice will also come from spiritual beings. Your purpose is to learn which voice lives on the dark side and is the loud chatty voice of the enemy. If you are not listening to any earthly spiritual advisors, then pray to God that you are not your own spiritual advisor for you have a fool for one. Pay attention to which shoulder the Darkside sits on for that will be where your negative thoughts are coming from. I pray that the power of God is working through you from within. Cherish the people God has sent to help you. TYJ

September 17

When anxiety, fear or worry steal your sleep or if your heart is feeling heavy from a failed relationship, know that you are unconditionally loved by God. He will always be there for you. Put all your troubles in His hands for God is bigger than anything you have going on in your life right now. All changes must start with you. Make the choice to improve. Set a course of action by not blaming anything or anyone for being the cause of your frustration. Your Darkside wants you to maintain your misery. Spiritual development starts with humility, showing responsibility and surrendering to God's will. Positive thinking starts with getting rid of your ego and pride. You start with hope that a spiritual life works. After a few small miracles you now have the faith that it does. TYJ

September 18

If you have a chance to be kind, show compassion or love. Do it. You may need to love them until they can learn to love themselves. Doing good for others always comes back to you in a positive way. Being a giver can have its drawbacks. There are takers who have no restrictions. They tend to prey on the givers. Karma will give them their just rewards. You need to pay attention to the soft gentle voice. It will do what's best to keep you safe. If you can spend time in silent meditation with God, do so. Time spent with God is better than facing the Darkside alone. Love the people who make it better for humanity to love within themselves. They have no idea how inspiring they are. Tonight, when looking at your day don't forget to forgive others. Thank God for what you have and pray for the needs of others. Your kind of people will always want what is best for you and you for them. TYJ

September 19

If you look for the good in yourself and another person your life will get better. You do not have to associate with everybody who wants to be in your life. You may have to set boundaries to protect yourself from harm. Not everyone will have your best interest at heart. By choosing to invite God into your life you will be filled with the blessings of being enough. You will not have to make them feel inadequate so you can feel good about yourself. You are the keeper of your own happiness. You are better off traveling alone than spending time with fake people whose lives are filled with drama. Make the choice to change. You may be the light that opens the door for others. Start with being kind to one person today. You may start an epidemic. Learn to love yourself and others unconditionally. TYJ

September 20

Do not grant anyone or any obsession total power over your happiness or health. If there is one thing you need to learn from your misguided unintentional departure from the truth it is that your health and wellbeing must come first. If you do not learn from your misjudgments, you are doomed to repeat them causing more mental and health issues. Do not let the opinions of others lower your feelings of self-worth. Through morning prayer and meditation, you will learn to stop judging other's mistakes. Lower your ego and have empathy for others. You recognize your own inaccuracies and become accountable for your blunders. You will gain a deeper understanding of the pain you have caused others. It is imperative that you get a God box and put everything you have no control over in it. Thinking minus action is procrastination. Write it down. You must or it will kill you bodily and mentally. Learn to help yourself by turning over one thing today. God is willing to help you. May you use Him now. Your wellbeing depends upon it. TYJ

September 21

When trudging the road to a happy destiny, it takes on the look of an uphill battle. Money is short and bills are high. Loneliness appears to be overwhelming. Do not fold under the pressure of the dark side for God will never give up on you. He knows what you are going through. You only must ask Him to join you in morning prayer and meditation. God never gives you more than you can handle when you seek His help. It will produce fear, frustration and anxiety on your own. With God on your side, it's a piece of cake. Just for today choose serenity. God gives you the respect and space to grow spiritually. He helps you to come to an understanding of his unconditional love. He has forgiven you for everything bad that you have ever done. It is time that you forgive yourself and others. Admit your wrongs and move on. What do you have to lose by setting boundaries? Start with controlling mental health abusing leeches. And maybe a manipulating narcissist or two. TYJ

September 22

When you choose to stop growing spiritually, chaotic thinking will become your normal way of life. Do not fear change, embrace it. Adjusting your thinking comes from the soft gentle voice. Ask God in your morning prayer and meditation what you can do for your struggling friends. Here is God's gift to you. For every 10 things you do for others, others will do for you. Your great reward will be your soul will receive the gifts of peace, love and joy. Do not wait for your life to get better before you help others. It will get better because you helped others. Be observant of what others accuse you of. That will tell you what you need to know about them. It may have nothing to do about you. TYJ

September 23

A deep friendship with a shallow person is difficult. You still need to show them that you care. You are strong and wise when you know your weaknesses. Learn from your mistakes. Anxiety comes from the false pretense that you must be perfect today. You get better with morning prayer and meditation by looking at your faults. Humble people know their flaws. Focus on today. Never regret anything from your past. It cannot be changed. Learn from your mistakes. It is okay not to have all the answers. You will have bad days. Ask for help. Most of all do not be a person who complains about everything. Appreciate everything. Even your difficulties. Do not be one of their victims. It will be useless to point out their deficiencies. They take no responsibility for their actions. It will be your fault. TYJ

September 24

Do not live under the false pretense that your life is going to be a soft easy journey. God gave us a free will to choose between the light or the dark side within us. Evil will be pulling you to a position to live with depraved motions. Get to the root of your occurrences and take responsibility for your actions. Ask God in morning prayer and meditation to remove these temptations. Action is a must. Throughout the day you will need to maintain your conscious contact with your Higher Power. Continue these positive feelings by choosing to put everything in God's hands. Trust Him. He will carry your burdens bringing you through the hard times. Thus, allowing you to live in peace and serenity. If you are new to this concept start with one troublesome small difficulty or affliction. You do control your own future events. Choose to make them special times. TYJ

September 25

Be vigilant, your Darkside is never going to give up. By starting your day with morning prayer and meditation, you will ensure your spirituality will show through by your attitude of contentment, confidence, positivity and open-mindedness. Do not let blaming, being petty or hateful be a part of your life today. Choose to be a happy, loving, kind person remaining at peace. With God in your life, you will remain calm while managing your thoughts, behaviors and emotions. Things will remain clear, logical and less stressful. Your goal for today is to live life to its fullest. Be at peace and love when helping others. You will possess a forgiving soul. Your Darkside will rear its ugly head in forms of anger and fearful aggressive displays of evil. There will be no peace of mind. No amount of sex, drugs, success or stuff will fill that hole in your soul. Love of life must come from the inside. All of this starts with your thinking. TYJ

September 26

By starting your day with morning prayer and meditation, you will be blessed with feelings of God's favor and protection. Receiving His hope, love, strength and comfort. Your life will become meaningful. Have a purpose and be restored with God's grace. This is an inside job. There is no knight on a white horse, going to slay your inner demons. Only the love of God and self can fill that empty hole in your soul. If you are fortunate, you will find a true friend that you can share all the chapters of your life with. There will be happy and sad times, even exciting occasions. This person will love you unconditionally throughout your entire existence. If no one appears right now know that God will always be there for you. He will lift the weight of your troubled life from your shoulders. He will keep you safe. Start with believing in yourself, right now. It makes no difference where you are at on your journey of life. It is easier to change your perception of a difficult or unpleasant set of circumstances then to change the condition of your situation. Your response can cause stress or be calming. Your choice. Do not wait for things to get easier. You are not guaranteed soft cushy life forces. TYJ

September 27

Anything you set your mind to is easily attainable if you are coinciding with God's will for you. You are in the effort business and God is in the "in charge of the results". You can save yourself a lot of stress and anxiety by not trying to control or manipulate the outcome. As you travel through this day, not everyone you meet is going to like you. People will say and do things you may not like. What is important is how you react to their perceived negativity. Ask God to bless them for hurting people want you to suffer also. Do not assume that it is always about you. Enjoy the people who do like you because it will help you to learn to like yourself. God's lesson for you today may be to learn to forgive others and yourself. Keep practicing until you get it right. Find a spiritual advisor who will listen to the ugly part of your past life. You have pushed your feelings deep down inside of you. Bring these dark secrets out into the open. The light of God will help to make them less painful. There will be people who may have to be forgiven. This needs to be done for your sanity and peace of mind. TYJ

September 28

God does give you more than you can handle by yourself. The more stressful your journey is the more essential that you turn to God. It is valuable that you slow your mind down with journaling and setting up an agenda. Look at what you can take care of and then do it. Do not stress out if you don't get everything done on your list. Some of us spend more time talking than doing. When writing down your thoughts there may be items that you have no control over. A very dear friend told me to draw a box around those items and give them to God. That simple move is an action. He can help turn your messages into victories. There is a useful prayer called The Serenity Prayer. When you are not okay ask God to please calm your mind by taking away your worries and anxieties. Sometimes you just need to allow others to be wrong. Make the choice to pay attention to the solution, to any mindset that is causing you anxiety. Visualize your ideal outcome. Breathe in God's love. Breathe out any fears. Choose not to react to negativity. Spend time with people who help bring God's light into your life. Send out love and forgiveness to all those who need it today. TYJ

September 29

80% of illnesses are the results of a lower resistance caused by physiological stress. Your physical health relates to your spiritual fitness. It does not make a lot of sense to overwork yourself to make lots of money. Then spend it to get your health back because you did not take care of yourself. Life is meant to be enjoyed. The benefits from starting your day with morning prayer and meditation are good health from less stress and anxiety. Which in turn leads to less colds, ailments and heart problems. Choose to allow God to be your new hope and light. It is wholesome to hang with people who make you laugh. If you want health and happiness, help others to find theirs. Your high moral principles and honesty will show up by how you treat people. The best gift you can give to anyone is kindness. Do not do it for the high yielding rewards. Do it because it is the right thing to do. TYJ

September 30

The stress of intense negative emotions like bitterness rage or envy can cause severe physical harm to the body. You can be hurt by how you treat others. The suffering you have caused them to endure by your words, behavior, abandonment or indifference Karma will bring back to you. Choose your thoughts and words wisely. Start your day with morning prayer and meditation. You will open new doors to help meet your needs and keep your expectations real. Who is directing your life? You or a power greater than yourself? Others can help you to confront your inner weaknesses, but God needs to be your main source of strength. Look for indicators of a life filled with spiritual fitness. You will display signs of positive thinking, optimism, harmony, humility and compassion. Most importantly you will have surrendered to a higher existence. Do not fear others who do not believe the same as you do. Each person must travel their own road to their happy destiny. TYJ

October 1

Become in tune with your body. When exhaustion sets in, rest. You want to go go, others need you. God is calling. I must be in service. Even God rested on the seventh day. You are of no good to anyone when you are running on empty. Take the time each week for a relaxing peaceful evening at home. Recovery takes time. Not everyone will appreciate the new you. There is that old vision of you that is stuck in their head. Keep working on becoming a better person. Make the choice of method and how fast in hopes they will appreciate the new you. Learn to recognize the full worth of what you have. Your happiness will be the consequences of your inner positive thoughts. The outcome will be better than you imagined. You have already survived the worst days that the Darkside threw at you. Do not let the dark side continue to influence your life. You can fix an absence of knowledge. A deficiency of common sense lasts forever. Let the light of God help to make the rest of your life a masterpiece. TYJ

October 2

God grant me the toughness to center my attention on being mindful of others. To serve God and be a force of his love. May you do God's work without being a victim or playing the martyr. You gain more knowledge from conflicts of anger and fighting your fears. Embrace your difficulties. Choose to learn your lessons gracefully. Be especially kind for God may have chosen you to give someone a special uplifting today. I ask that my friends and family feel loved. May your worries and fears be blessed by God. May you never underestimate what God is doing for you. He has blessed you numerous times. May you feel His favor and protection. When doing your morning prayer and meditation, make the choice to take God with you when facing your life situations. He can calm any storm you may be facing today. Maintain an open mind for your thoughts are not always correct. Allow God to extend his values and peace into your life. He will drain you of your hurt and hostilities. TYJ

October 3

Do not try to control or make your goals happen. Relax, let go and let God. Life is an echo of what you send out you get back. You will receive favorable by sending out good. Your choice. At the end of the day all that matters is that you did all the excellence you could for your loved ones. Giving everything you had no control over to God. You embrace the good going on during your time on Earth. You pray for the wisdom to know the difference. Your old negative past will not last forever. Choose to close the door on it. Start a new chapter in your life. In morning prayer and meditation ask God to join you on your new positive journey. Just for today you will not judge, condemn or blame others for any misfortunes going on in your life. You are kind to others. Your past has taught you the sensation of a particular experience and how it feels to be mistreated, lonely, shameful and full of regrets. Helping others to find the solution to their misfortunes is your responsibility. While still being careful of the bullshitters. You forgive anyone who has ever done you harm. TYJ

October 4

Life is about accepting everything on life's terms. Struggles are a part of your existence so is thinking positive, telling the truth and having faith in God. Every morning when you wake up God will be writing a new page to your story. He does not require your help on how this day will pan out. He does necessitate you to start your day with morning prayer and meditation to find out what His purpose is for you. Learn to trust that soft gentle voice within you. Only you can dance to your music. Do not let others tell you what songs to listen to. He is pleased when your page is full of good deeds done for others. He is really displeased when everything is about you and how everyone owes you. The choice is yours. Do you want positive or negative karma? Seek to gain the knowledge from your lessons needed to obtain a purpose for your survival. Stop whining about why this is happening to you. Why is a management question and you are not in management. God is. Forgive others. Master the art of loving yourself. TYJ

October 5

A true friend is someone you can trust and is happy for you. Supports your relationships with others, tells you the truth when you screw up and praises you when you do good. They know all about your past and still choose to love you unconditionally. No one is innocent for there were times in your life that you did not make the best choices. That special someone will help you to become a better person than you were yesterday. Do not fear, God is providing guidance. You are in his plans. You will have suggested alternatives to learn on the way. In morning prayer and meditation, God will tell you to stop worrying and give your fears to Him. Have faith for there is nothing you have done or will do that He has not already forgiven you for. Is there anything going to happen that with His help the both of you cannot handle together? Keeping a receptive mind will prove to be advantageous. Do not leave God in your meditation room. Invite Him to join you in your adventures today. TYJ

October 6

If you are doing kind deeds so others will like you. Stop!! Learn to respect and love yourself for who you are. Not what you think others value of you is. God's will for you is to do random acts of kindness. It is the right thing to do. Let go and let God means just that. Stop the need to control others and circumstances. Look at why your life is so difficult. God uses pain and suffering to get your attention. He is teaching you to focus on Him. Your life will become blessed by the results of right thinking known as an attitude adjustment. An occasional meltdown is okay. Just do not unpack your negative thinking and take up residence. Stop punishing yourself for past deficiencies. You did not know any better back then. The problem is if you keep doing them now that you do know better. Does the Darkside still control you? God does say I have to love you, but I do not have to invite you to my Halloween party. Your actions tell us who you are, not what you tell us. TYJ

October 7

Find the good in your life. Trudging the road to a happy destiny requires looking at the positive side of life. If you honestly seek God, He will find true happiness and serenity for you. Smile, listen, play, love and most importantly help somebody today. Let them see your inner strength. Be vulnerable but cautious. They may never admit their mistakes or see their defects or apologize for anything. Love them anyway and pray for them. They are the sick ones. The fact that you are changing, growing and healing causes fear in them. They are hanging on to their ego. Let go of the idea that you must be liked by them. Learn to let others feel the afflictions of the bad choices they make are on them. Stop taking on the agony for them. Sensitive people love additionally. They suffer more at the hands of the insensitive. The Darkside of life will have them wishing bad to come to others, even death. It shows how emotionally sick and evil they really are. TYJ

October 8

You will have a positive impact on the world around you if you are living in the solution. A program of action. If not, you remain a part of the problem. Get rid of the notion that reacting with feelings of anger, injustice, ingratitude and belittling people are a sign of strength. Make a difference. You are one choice away from changing your life. Cause and effect rule the Universe. For every yin there is a yang. Start every morning with positive prayer and meditation to keep from trying to solve today's problems with yesterday's negative thinking. Visualize your life as you wish it to be. Your solutions will improve drastically. Make the choice to distance yourself from adverse people. Everything you need to survive and prosper is within you. Thus, obtaining peace of mind and confidence. Let go of the idea that everyone must conform to your way of thinking. You may be braver and wiser because of the tough sequence of negative events you have endured. True feelings of joy come from how you view your life situations. They are either discoveries to conform to a positive standard of living or lessons. Others must learn their own insights on their own schedule. If they choose to do so. TYJ

October 9

Start your day by looking at your joys and counting your blessings. Claiming good health will bring spiritual and physical wellness to you. Giving you the mindset that is a privilege to be alive and able to cope with life situations. Give thanks to God for everything going on in your life today. Having gone through the worst of times yourself you now want what's best for others. The struggles of your past have helped to make you the strong, caring person you are today. You are grateful for the people who enhance your life now. God sends people to help you escape the past. Instead of spending time dwelling on mistakes look at them as lessons you needed to learn and move on. View them as dead and buried. People may fail to see your self-worth, do not be one of them. Drugs or sexual encounters are not the answers to relieving the pain or failed relationships. Doing the same old stuff only causes fearful frustration and anger. Trust God to heal your emotional experiences by relieving you of any worries, resentments or anxieties. TYJ

October 10

Doubt, worry and anxiety are opposing forces to stilling the loud chattering monkey voice of your mind. Your lower power wants you emotionally or spiritually dead. He does not care which one. He has victorious feelings of accomplishment when you are both. By starting your day with morning prayer and meditation you can defeat the Darkside. What you think you become so be careful of what you provide your mind. It believes all the negative BS you furnish it. Getting your intense feelings and processing your life experiences while living in a life filled with meaning and purpose requires you to get your s*** together. Looking at it with rose colored glasses is not beneficial. You may only be capable of working on one small item from that pile. In the long run it may turn out to be the start of one giant step towards peace and serenity. You need to plant positive flowers in your garden (mind) and stop growing weeds. Create a positive world around you by attracting people who practice your new way of thinking. Remain strong. Instead of giving into negative urges, take God with you wherever you go today. Allow Him to help you. TYJ

October 11

Anxiety is better explained as self-centered counterproductive worry. It is your way of telling God that you don't think He can handle your life situations. Meditation is a practice of allowing yourself to feel comfortable with whatever happens in your life today. By affirming constructive attributes and optimistic ideas, visualize the person you want to be. Do not brag to impress others. Let your actions do it for you. Unless of course you are filled with rage and condemnation then make the choice to change. Your Darkside is a bad example for anyone who is recovering from their addictions. You do not get to judge us or we you. No one is flawless. With morning prayer and meditation, you will receive the gift of humility and selflove. Thus, supporting you with the opportunity to start working on transforming yourself into the person God intended you to be. You will be correcting years of negative thinking. Start with changing one angry outburst into an apology. One evil deed into an act of kindness. Let go of a situation you have no control over. One small step towards a positive life will turn into a giant leap towards a better you. Be patient. It took many years to get this negative. TYJ

October 12

Give yourself permission to be human. The first part of change is accepting that you can be controlling and possessing addictive behaviors. Denial will be your biggest challenge for your Darkside does not want you to become a better person. Has your lower power convinced you that He does not exist? Having a positive outlook on life does not mean that everything will work out in your favor. With morning prayer and meditation and God in your life you will maintain the faith needed to be okay with all your past life situations. Do not give power to your negative thoughts about your past. Forgive yourself as you did not know any better. Because of the person you are today, experience has taught you the truth. Have no regrets of your past discretions for they help to form who you are today. Maintain peace of mind is an essential part of life. Having humility affords you plenty of opportunity to be grateful. Thus, allowing patience to enter your life. Smile, you are on God's camera. TYJ

October 13

Believing you do not deserve good is a sign of low self-esteem. Affirm you are a kind loving person deserving of God's goodness. Breathe in God's loving kindness and breathe out negativity. Take the good with the bad while concentrating on having an awesome day. Give to those in need. Do not give to the point that you are being used. Trust in God. Do not be naïve about the users and takers. Be a good listener. Do not lose your own identity. With morning prayer and meditation, you will learn to soar with the eagles. Find new solutions to today's problems. Focus on the Light around you not the Darkness. You are told to stop trying to control others by forcing things to go your way. Do not lose sight of the fact that you do have control over which endeavors you choose to put an effort in to and your attitude. God's guidance for you will be what works out without your assistance. Be honest with others even it if demolishes their misinterpretations of a correct sensory input. There will be consequences for both your positive and negative actions. Choose wisely. TYJ

October 14

Life does not need to be perfect to be joyous. A few good friends who love you for who you are and make you feel that your craziness is plausible. They are a blessing sent by God. Don't be too hard on yourself. The Darkside has sent people to dish out your bad karma. You control the amount by your actions. Make the choice to travel in the light by being kind and loving to all. You will receive only good back. The distinct control you have is how you react to life situations. Others have the right to set boundaries without us doing rageful retaliation while playing the role of the victim. You have absolutely no control over others. So, stop trying, learn to create. When you travel on the Darkside you will constantly need to express regret and be remorseful for your actions. When traveling in God's light and doing His will you do not have to be apologetic for having Him in your life. Be a forgiving soul and seek God's love. TYJ

October 15

Guilt and shame are feelings. Feel them and make good the harm you have caused others. Release them by asking God to remove these defects of character. The Darkside wants you to feel guilty and shameful while being critical of others. Wishing bad to happen to anyone is Evil. This is caused by living in fear with traits of greed, spitefulness and narcissistic tendencies. You can rationalize and justify your behavior all you want. It is simply listening to the negative, loud chatty monkey voice on your shoulder. Have you ever wondered what the demons look like that are occupying your mind, just waiting for someone to upset your day? Self-control and calmness are the positive features needed to keep your emotions from influencing your ability to handle life situations peacefully. You will be better equipped to face your evil by starting your day with morning prayer and meditation thus defeating these feelings of failure. Do not be afraid to be yourself. People will love you for who you will turn out to be. If you continually work to improve yourself your happiness starts with you living in the presence of your higher power. Choose to make this a happy day. TYJ

October 16

On your toughest days in life, breathe God in while breathing insecurity, anxiety and fear out. Conquering fear will be on of your most noted achievements. Second will be walking away from anything or anyone who ruins your soul. Take God with you in all your battles. He will help to bring good behavior while practicing your program of action. When living on the Darkside you will be under the false pretense that all human beings other than yourself are responsible for your love and emotional state of wellbeing. You are then violating one of the irrefutable laws of the universe. You and you alone are responsible for your own happiness. Start with loving yourself. If you feel you don't deserve this love you have a tool called "acting as if". Until you can love yourself you have nothing to offer anyone else other than stuff. With morning prayer and meditation, you can face your defects and confront your ego driven beliefs which manifest your inner darkness. TYJ

October 17

Trying is working on yourself from the outside. When you "let go and let God", you are working on yourself from the inside. Then miracles can happen. If you are accepting yourself as you are, nothing changes. You begin your miracle when you choose to become a better person. It starts with a nightly inventory of your day and morning prayer and meditation to obtain a conscious contact with God throughout the day. Learn to let your day flow without contriving anything. If a door does not open let it go. Neither friendship, love nor jobs can be compelled. It is what it is. Choose what you fight for and make sure it is worthwhile. You have total responsibility to heal yourself. No one can do it for you. Be grateful for your story of hardships from bad choices. By redeveloping yourself you will transform the world around you also. All that pain and suffering made you the strong, confident useful person you are today. TYJ

October 18

You know you are in a presence of God when your life is centered, quiet, relaxed and you are feeling good about what you are doing. When your life is in an emotional state of being, off centered or out of balance focus on the practice of bringing God back into your life. Choose to take Darkside's depriving you of the confidence and hope and use them as steppingstones to turn them into positives. Do not become discouraged from past disappointments. Start with letting things happen the way God intended them to be instead of what you think they should be. Stick with people who bring you joy into your life not craziness and drama. Start living with a positive purposeful life. Growing from within, not how much stuff can I buy. Choose to fill that big empty hole in your soul with God's love. Your goal for today should be to become a better person than you were yesterday. Being flawed is a part of life but never let it cause you to feel less than. Always give it your best. Remember love is what you do more than what you say. TYJ

October 19

The busier and increasingly hectic your day is the more you need to seek God in your life. If saying to God, "where were you today?" He will say, "my child, you did not ask". Knock and the door will be opened. Seek and you shall find. Be brave enough to query for God will be pleased to be requested to join you in your mess called life. By letting go you will receive the gift of freedom. He will show you how blessed you are. You will stop wondering, obsessing and clinging to anger or fear. You will gain the knowledge of knowing everything will work out for God is leading you to your purpose in life. The world needs more peacemakers. The Darkside has you believing that wrong looks like right. Soon everything will make sense. Going down the scariest path is the most rewarding. Your best results come from making better choices. True happiness comes from your own actions of doing right. When it is all said and done God will show you how to be humble of heart. Do not allow others to bring chaos or the Darkside into your house. You are love and love is what you do. TYJ

October 20

Do you practice our code of love and tolerance by allowing others to have their own point of view? Their opinions count. Let them be happy in their own way although it may differ from yours. They may say things that hurt you. It is their reality not yours. Do not let your past experiences go to waste. Nothing can be substantiated for all that knowledge that comes from screwing up. Everything you have today is because of God's grace. Be thankful for the good and use the bad to grow for your richest wealth is wisdom and patience. May your faith in God prevail to bring laughter into your soul. Choose to stay strong during your storm. Do not let your heart be hardened from the past rocky roads. Let love be your answer. Do not try to be who you are not just to please others. With morning prayer and meditation, practice being honest today. Choose to stay away from perfect for you will not reach that goal. Excellent is good enough. The world is a better place when you rejoice in your quietness, realizing that you are lacking nothing. Always be forgiving when others insult you. Show love and kindness thus turning pain and sadness into joy. Know that things have a way of working out for the best when given the time needed. TYJ

October 21

People walking away from your life may have nothing to do with you. Sometimes God removes people because they will only hinder you on your next level. People come into your life for a reason, a season or a lifetime. Know the reason for every person in your life. If they have served their purpose let them go. A sign of maturity is walking away when people threaten your peace of mind, self-respect or self-worth. The word self means you cannot find these attributes in others. It can only come from within. Keep moving forward assisting others to evolve. Your supporting another not only affects their life but the lives of those around them. Providing aid to one person at a time is how we make the world a better place to live in. Be happy in this moment and every juncture. Start your day with prayer and meditation. It is important how you respond, not what they did. Reacting in hostility can be injurious both psychologically and physically. It may be an adverse sign of the Darkside within you. Put everything in God's hands today. He will help to carry your burdens and quell your fears. TYJ

October 22

You are here to learn. Make a difference in your life by starting your day with prayer and meditation. Give birth to a new way of thinking powerful thoughts from the light. Stop focusing on what others did to you and concentrate on the love and kindness God has bestowed upon you. Do not accept the restraints of fear, frustration and hateful angry thoughts manufactured by the Darkside. These will cause you to feel broken, rejected, depressed, ashamed and obsessed with feelings of being unworthy of God's love. Remember the word self as in self-worth comes from your Higher Power. The Darkside can only offer stuff. Reject these restrictions and make a difference in your life by thinking powerful positive thoughts. Stop focusing on blaming others for your misfortunes. Do not let your emotions get the best of you. Thus, providing you have a long way to go on your journey of becoming a better person. Check out the people you meet today. Either they are here to help you or you them. Your purpose in life for today will be to teach or learn, maybe even both. With God's guidance you can be victorious for He will heal your soul and take away your worries. All you must do is ask. TYJ

October 23

Your best answers to life situations will come through prayer and meditation. Prayer and change go hand in hand. Recovery from the Darkside will happen for you signs of less judging, outer chaos and fear. Negative life situations are not going to stop happening. God will supply you with the strength and ability to remain calm during the storm. Know that better days are coming after you have learned your lesson. It is time for a yearly reminder of doing our nightly inventory. Ask yourself, was I resentful, nasty rude or angry? Was I selfish or dishonest? Was I afraid, worried or living in anxiety? Do I owe an apology? Have I kept something to myself which should be discussed with someone immediately? Was I kind and loving towards all or was I thinking of myself most of the time? Was I contemplating on what I could do for others? What could I have done better? Ask God for forgiveness and inquire what corrective measures should be taken. God forgive me for my failings today. Help me to live thy will better tomorrow. Guide me to make my relationships right. TYJ

October 24

When asking God for help you must do your part by changing any imperfections that you can. Your innermost thoughts reflect both your positive and negative sides. Inventory and journaling will help you to review even your smallest deficiencies. With morning prayer, meditation and God's help, you are bigger than any problem you will face today. Your ego (The Darkside) will give you the perception that being right is more important than being loving. May God help you to become humble enough to see that you may be wrong sometimes. There is no way you can be right all the time. Pain appears to be God's best weapon for getting your attention. It takes a big person to admit they are wrong. You carry a lot of baggage with you from your past. Knowing you are powerless over your addictions goes a long way in helping you. You will achieve positive attributes of love, good health and finding the truth. Make the choice to let them go. God can fill that empty space with his healing love to change you with positive solutions. Please I beg of you let the miracle happen. TYJ

October 25

Just for today, may God take from your mind all turmoil, stress and tiredness. Stop living in the past, fearing change and putting yourself down. God loves you for who you are although after a period he will request that you work on becoming a better person. Overthinking brings excessive worry into your life. Positive thinking serves two purposes. You expect the most advantageous to happen in your life. You also accept whatever is happening to be superior for you. With morning prayer and meditation, your life can be filled with excitement, meaning and delight. It is time to quit trying to please everyone else for God has a reason and a purpose for your life. He is glad you are alive so never stop trying to please him. The stuff the dark side promises you is not what is exemplary for you. The people you meet and the memories you make are precious. Treasure them. TYJ

October 26

Today is a great day to be thankful for all the assets God has blessed you with. Start with training your mind to see joy in all your efforts. How you perceive your journey will go a long way in making it a delightful one. Good thoughts bring desired results. Celebrate your growth and recovery. Take God with you in all aspects of your life. Do not let what you think should happen stand in the way of God's plan. When in the middle of your mess don't forget to thank God and the people who help cause it. They were the ones who made you the strong person you are today. Be grateful for the lessons learned. Live the life you were given for today instead of the one you wish you had. Stuff will happen today because of choices you have made in the past. Observe what life is asking you to learn and make an honest effort to make better choices in the future. Karma and acceptance will play a big part in this. TYJ

October 27

List five things you must be grateful for today. Thank God for these. Look at anything negative going on in your life. Ask God to remove these for He will once you have learned your lessons. Do not be afraid to shake up the Evil existing here on Earth. Because of bad choices and Karma, everything flourishing in your existence is meant to be. Put your trust in God, learn from your mistakes and move on. Focus on yourself to become stronger. God will guarantee that your life will get healthier. Do not allow anyone to make you feel less than. Do not be desperate enough to beg anyone to be in your life. Relieve yourself of nervous tensions by allowing God to help you with relationship choices. God values every human being in society as equals. The people who think they are better than you are only fooling themselves. The narcissists of the planet have two choices. Either die serving the Darkside or get down on their knees and ask God for forgiveness. Their selfish pride and ego are of no service to humanity. TYJ

October 28

May you take the opportunity God offers and demonstrate everything good and worthwhile in your life today. Do not let little messes spoil how blessed you are. May God give you the power, energy and goodness to make your lives and the lives of others a tremendous experience. Pay attention to who increases your energy in the world. That is who you should embrace. The only person you can bring into alignment with the Cosmos is yourself. Count your blessings and practice acts of love and kindness. Out of your emotional pain and suffering will emerge the strong person you are meant to be. It is wise to protect your Spiritual Psychic from negative people. They represent the Darkside. They are sent to ruin your day. Make the choice to look forward to a beautiful day. With morning prayer and meditation ask God to help you choose your actions wisely. You will learn to replace fear with prayer, gratitude instead of whining and the power to never give up. You do not have control over consequences caused by the poor choices from the past. Karma (Golden Rule) will be judging all your maneuvers today. TYJ

October 29

Serenity begins with the exercise of self-discipline and guarding against selfish gratification. Morning prayer and meditation, along with performing acts of moderation and thoughtfulness, will help you to scrutinize the tongue and improve your temperament. Do not react to every thought for our first impulse is to react with negativity. Being sorry for your random acts of negativity have no positive outcome unless you make the choice to change your behavior by giving yourself the gift of forgiveness. Love yourself enough to take positive action and gain back the trust of others. Keep your thoughts positive. Do not grant life situations the power to overwhelm you. Make calming the loud chatty monkey voice in your mind a priority. Do not allow how you think it should happen influence your actions. Remember God has got this. Let Him help you through any adversity you may endure today. If no one told you that you are loved, essential and more stalwart than you think. I am telling you now that you are. TYJ

October 30

Hurting people hurt others. You cannot change them although you can help them. They must choose to reconstruct their lives and find God. If not, you may have to make the choice to be around other people. Through morning prayer and meditation, you can make that transition to the Light for life is supposed to be fun. Turn down those loud chatty monkey voices that shame and judge you. The soft gentle voice will show you how you can be at peace within yourself. Choose to be playful and feel appreciated by hanging with people who enjoy, respect and value you. Which in turn causes you to feel loved, prestigious and happy. You are meant to be independent, not needy, for you must feel alright within yourself before you can be okay with anyone else. Being judgmental means one simple thing. You are traveling with the Dark side. Please make the choice to travel in the Light. The Universe can reward you with positive thoughts when you reach an understanding of how it works. Stop looking to the Darkside to support your wrong doings by rationalizing and justifying your negative behavior. TYJ

October 31

Your power lies in how you respond to what is happening in your life. Taking action in fear or anxiety is contrary to trusting in God. It may cause you to suffer from adverse psychological effects. You will not be able to go back and fix everything you did wrong. With morning prayer and meditation, you can start your day with God. This will enable you to choose your words wisely and therefore not offend as many people. Today is a new day and you will have opportunities for a fresh new start. Choose to be positive and get your thinking right first thing in the morning. You can choose to hang on to your old ideas and stay mired in your Darkness. Do not allow your thoughts to tell you that you are not beautiful, smart or important. Be cautious. If someone treated you badly once they will be inclined to do it again. By you not accepting their bad behavior puts their negativity back on them. By their actions you will know them. They choose to remain in the dark. Learn to understand yourself and you will master the art of self-love and caring for others. You might just as well get used to the idea that not everything is going to turn out as you planned. Acceptance of God's will instead of yours will go a long way towards serenity. Your choice. Craziness or peace. TYJ

November 1

It is with gratitude and appreciation that I declare that I am blessed with everything I need. I thank God for the difficulties and challenges that have strengthened and promoted my spiritual growth. I set out my plan for today, wrote it down, took a deep breath and let go of the obsession to control. Trying to direct people's behavior will only lead to feelings of hopeless frustration. Doing the task and turning it over to God is my part in the outcome. The consequences will be based on my motives. Strong intentions good results, bad aspirations crummy consequences. Karma will always play a part in the development. If my affect did not consist of advantageous qualities yesterday, I need to look at my effort. There are consequences for dreadful actions or procrastination. I must strive to do better for it is never too late to reverse my devious actions and start my day over. Spirituality is all about change. If I alter my thoughts, I will modify my world. I will remain patient while God reveals my purpose in life. If I want to be loved and respected, I must show deep affection and esteem to others. TYJ

November 2

Happiness is contingent on your spiritual condition. Not on the right relationship or a new car, right clothes or hairdo condition. It is based on your inner psychic, peace and purpose. Your highest priority is to be loving to yourself and others. All the other things will be afforded to you based on your needs not necessarily on your wants. God will provide everything you warrant on your journey through life. Your sense of wellbeing will always be about learning to love yourself not your intimate material objects. Stop overthinking your problems and give them to God. Reflect positive thoughts. Know that having a bad day does not convey you are having a bad life. Just because s*** happens does not signify you have to wallow in it. Make the most out of this day and you will be happy. Learn to accept people for who they are. Bad traits and all. Not on who you want them to be. Otherwise, they will never reach your standards and will always be a disappointment to you. Just for today know that God sees them and you as good enough. He does rejoice when you make the choice to get better and to be grateful for what you have. Both will go a long way in helping you to be happier. TYJ

November 3

Through morning prayer and meditation, you will exercise being loving and humble while practicing patience. You learn to speak your own mind by not agreeing with others to maintain peace. Never allow anyone to disrespect the boundaries you have set up for your own tranquility. This word no takes on a new meaning. It is a full sentence. You no longer react to negative thoughts knowing what a privilege it is that God selected you to comfort others. You choose to run your own life while confirming to God's will for you. You provide aid to those deemed necessary along with taking care of your own wants. You find a life that best suits you. Providing aid is the greatest gift you can bestow upon another. Learn to love yourself enough to become willing to change for the better. The Darkside can only offer you stuff. Craving more is not a blessing. We buy too much. Eat too much to fill that big empty hole in our soul. You have friends who will walk the road with you. You alone must find a God of your understanding to fill that empty space. TYJ

November 4

The benefits of morning prayer and meditation are forever growing. You start with guiding your thoughts to see the positivity in everything. You will have more serenity and tolerance along with less fear and anger when you stop complaining. You become aware of the fact that most of your stress comes from the way you feel about what is happening. Not the way life really is. Adjusting your thinking will remove a lot of your frustration. You will gain a quiet courage. Sanity will return. Your sense of purpose and direction will expand. Relationships with family and friends will improve. If you want peace and tranquility in your life, make the decision to change. The universe will make it happen. God is giving you three things to do today. 1st watch your impressions when you are alone for dangerous emotional unpleasantries, either real or imagined, start with just one negative thought. 2nd mind your tongue when you are with others, negative hurting words cannot be unsaid. 3rd never give up the fight, trust in God. He has your best interest in mind 24/7. TYJ

November 5

Do not waste time trying to be who others want you to be. It is by your sadness that you will learn what real happiness is. You do not need a lot of friends. Just real ones who love you for who you are without trying to change you to fit their needs. Not everyone is meant to be in your life. Stop begging them to stay. Let go of your past for there is nothing you can do to change it. Make apologies when needed. Pay the money back. Today make the choice to create a better world to live in. Loneliness should not be a prerequisite when wanting to add someone to your life. When you display characteristics of being needy you end up driving them away. When you make the choice to add someone to your life material things are nice. Look for someone who will give you loyalty, honesty and their undivided attention. The answers will come to you from the inside when you seek God to fill that hole in your soul. With morning prayer and meditation, your wants will coincide with your needs. Your Truths will become clearly visible to you as you travel your Spiritual journey. TYJ

November 6

If you disagree with someone's lifestyle you do not need to fear or hate them. If you love someone you do not have to agree with everything they believe or do. You do not have to compromise convictions to be compassionate. Friendships need to be deeper than gossip. More open than talking about life struggles and how to overcome them. With a real friend you do not have to pretend your life is all together. Rather than asking God why? Take the time to see what lessons are hidden in your pain. The pain will stop when you have completed your learning process. Miracles do happen, keep the faith. It starts with morning prayer and meditation and finding out God's will and purpose for you. Real friends will support your goals and believe in you. Be cautious of people who do not respect your boundaries or feelings. Learn to stand up for yourself. Saying No does not make you self-centered. Learn to let go of old ideas and face change openly. Life is forever modifying. Go with the flow. Look for the best in others. The world has enough critics. TYJ

November 7

Bring meaning and peace into your life and relationships. What the other person did does not relieve you of your responsibility for your actions. They may have been critical of you or undermined your chosen purpose in life. They reacted to their faults and perceptions, not yours. Tell them how you feel without being discourteous. Do not add on to your bitterness by stubbornly hanging on to resentments. You made the choice to react in anger. Sometimes life's lessons are hard. They also made you the strong person you are today. Do not throw away the good God is presenting to you by hanging on to rage or hate. Through morning prayer and meditation, you can learn to embrace a new way of thinking. Free of fear and anxiety. God did not create you to live in misery. He wants you to be joyful, loving and kind. God used every hardship you endured and all the pain you have suffered to help you reach that goal. Today when confronted with fear, breathe in God's love. Breathe out the Darkside's negative thoughts. You know that loud chatty monkey voice of your mind. TYJ

November 8

You found power in the negative feelings that rage, intimidation or money gave when hoping to control others. As you grow in your spirituality with morning prayer and meditation you learn that God is the one true Power in your life and the lives of others. You gain knowledge from your mistakes and learn to appreciate the good in others forgiving them when the obligation arises. You must free yourself of the quest to control others. Do you keep meeting the same type of people that you can control? What is your lesson? Learn it. Move on. Meet a better quality of friends. Controlling people are themselves weak individuals. Not powerful. Release yourself of the shame of what could have been. If only you had done things differently. You forgive yourself by not becoming a hostage of your past. If you do not like the way your life is today, make that choice to change it. The Darkside domineers you with stuff. Your peace and serenity can only come from the inside. Trust your instincts. Your gift of happiness comes from lowering your expectations of others and being grateful for what you have. TYJ

November 9

When feeling the need to condemn others, do a quick inventory of your own shortcomings. Ask God for forgiveness of your defects and then you can start on the other person's flaws by praying for them to want to change. You have but one life. Do not waste it being critical or judgmental. Be proud of who you are and what you will become for it will get better. With morning prayer and meditation, make the choice to take at least one risk. You will achieve the feeling of Serenity. You will find peace of mind by staying focused. Ask the Universe to help you achieve your goals. Start with believing in yourself. At the end of the day know that you did the best that you chose to do. Do you realize how far you have come on your journey? It took a lot of work after you made the choice to pull yourself out of the Darkside. Your life will always be complicated. Choose to be happy right now. TYJ

November 10

It is important to feel good about yourself whether others approve of you or not. You will not be accepted by every single person. Being consumed with fear and anger will cause you to project those negative feelings on to others. You must heal your wounds. The love of a few good friends will help to carry you through your healing process when times are tough. Ask God to help lighten your burdens when they appear too heavy to carry on your own. God does use others to help during these adverse conditions. Seek God's guidance to help with self-love. That will be your biggest asset. The holidays are coming soon. You do not have to spend time with family members who are not good for your emotional wellbeing. Anxiety is God's way of telling you of potential danger. Not all fear is bad for you. Learn to know the difference. TYJ

November 11

Do not accept that anyone having a lousy day is your fault. Understand that their crummy day is theirs. Do not try to fix the choice they made to live on the Darkside. It is not your responsibility to keep others from growing through their pain. Because of choices they made Karma will have them paying particular attention to what they will draw into their lives. God does use distress to get their attention so they can gain the needed knowledge to find Him. Help them to change their thoughts about the situation. It can improve their spirituality with morning prayer and meditation. Pray with them to seek God's guidance on how to handle these adverse situations. This is not rocket science. If you focus on the Light and live a supportive lifestyle, Karma will bring these approving qualities into your life. Your choice. Gifts may be hard to come by this year. Show your family how much you care. This may be God's way of providing us with gifts of love and kindness. Give personal gifts of humility, acceptance, and joy. Thank a veteran today. TYJ

November 12

If you don't like the direction your life is going, change it. God loves honesty over perfection. Worry will not change it. It is another form of prayer. It tells God you don't think He can handle your life situations. When in doubt close your eyes and say, "God I need a little help down here. Thank you". Your negative forms of irrational judgment from the Darkside destroys today's peace. You have the power to make the choice to develop a new way of reflecting. Focus on a life filled with gratitude. You will want to block out any negative reactions of the unkind aspect of your mind. It starts with morning prayer and meditation. Be patient, talk to God. Your spiritual advisor can help implement a plan using affirmation. Start with, "Damn I am good. God loves me". All the love from others in the world will not work until you make the choice to receive it. Pray for the power to heal. You can stop hurting others. God may have removed someone from your life because He has seen all this person's conversations and actions. Happiness starts with being grateful for all the painful lessons and benefits you have received. TYJ

November 13

Do not let your contentment depend upon how others treat you or what they can buy for you. The Darkside says, "Everything will fall into place when you possess everything you desire." The Darkside can only offer you stuff. The Light says, "Be appreciative of what you have right now". You will find peace and serenity which in turn brings good health. The most beautiful components you have are the gracious people who have brought you happiness and fond memories. Be satisfied with the good. Choose to work on your defects. Stop being a people pleaser. Gain the knowledge to stay in the moment by setting your own standards for emotional gratification. Learn when to say no if the situation does not fit your norm. Start with accepting yourself. Staying in the now will help to heal you. Do not let your past control your future. Focusing on the negative part of your past will lead to anger and sadness. You will need to step out of your comfort zone. Your initial action must be morning prayer and meditation. Take the first step towards seeking God for your gratification. Choose a spiritual advisor who has gone through the maximum difficult situations. They will have the largest amount of empathy and knowledge. TYJ

November 14

With morning prayer and meditation, you can practice the presence of God by doing what he asks you to do. Knowledge is of no use if you do not live within His guidance. Real love of self will eventually lead to clean living. You are showing signs of improvement for you are less hypercritical of others. You hang on to fewer resentments and have reduced chaos and confusion in your life. You have a newfound faith therefore allowing you to react to every situation with less fear and anxiety. You now see things as they are and have stopped living in your dream world. You love others and will make the expedition with them. You know they must travel their own road to freedom from the Darkside. The choice must be theirs. You know that life will always have its ups and downs. You are more productive for you have learned to slow down, taking periods of rest when needed for both the mind and body. You put on your suit of armor dressed in love, compassion, and kindness to do battle against the Darkside. You have a newfound purpose in life and are ready to give it away to others. You give no one permission to be critical of you. You see yourself as a worthwhile person. You view your life as breathtakingly glamorous. TYJ

November 15

God allows bad actors to come into your life. They help mold you into the strong individual that He would like you to be. When others treat you badly it is critical that you do not retaliate. It says more about the angry, hateful people they are then it does about you. It is not selfish to take care of yourself. Set boundaries. Help others. It is imperative that you learn from your mistakes. Give your power to the solution or you will continually keep making them. Learn not to take everything personally for expectations causes feelings of entitlement. Gratitude is God's way of saying trust everything to Me. You can learn more by remaining silent and watching what is going on then reacting to the negativity of the Darkside. People's actions, not words, will always reveal how they are on the inside. When someone hurts you take the opportunity to help it change you. Pray for them to want to change. Thank God for the new person you have become. Pass any new knowledge you may receive on to others. Just for today you will treat others with dignity and respect. TYJ

November 16

Just for today, treat everyone you meet with kindness and respect. First because it's the right thing to do. Secondly it comes back to you. You will reap what you sow. You receive great benefits from starting your day with morning prayer and meditation. Enjoy your individual experiences during the good times. More importantly gain wisdom from your encounters when life gives you opportunities for growth. God will never allow you to be in situations that He and you cannot handle together. Seek His guidance. When you see life as a blessing it will become one. You base your decisions on love and common sense, not fear. You are unique, loved, and worthy of respect. You walk away from people who do not feel the same about you. They will poison your soul. They do practice a form of selflove when traveling to the Darkside. It is called being selfish and self-centered. Your happiness depends on your ability to stay away from them. Being forgiving and grateful will help you to be a better person than you were yesterday. TYJ

November 17

Forget the lies that tell you that you must be perfect and that everyone has to like you. Shoot for excellence. Start with loving yourself and knowing that God loves you. He has forgiven you for everything no matter who you have hurt or what you have done. Make the choice of forgiving yourself, an enduring position. Many of the things you suffered through made you the strong and compassionate person you are today. Along with the ability and willingness to help others. Just for today look forward to any negative challenges the Darkside may present you with. Setting boundaries does not give you permission to be rude or nasty. They will help you to withstand the pressures of your day and the ability to show mercy. Circumstances may get complicated because of bad choices made in the past. Pause, take a deep breath. Ask God to help you with any goals you seek to accomplish. TYJ

November 18

Do not invite drama and negativity into your life. You may not openly say it, but it is a part of your subconscious makeup. One good thing is if you learned it, you can unlearn it. With morning prayer and meditation, you can change your thoughts to positive action. It becomes your new habit which will allow your whole character to make the change. There will be times when you feel like quitting. Never give up on your quest to become a better person. Letting go and letting God is a goal you must learn to live by. Take nothing personally for when you perceive others as attacking you it is always everything about them and nothing about you. Do not react with negativity. Stay away from unnecessary conflict. Your Darkside wants you lonely and negative. Take the time to be kind to one person today. You may be the only one who does. Make a difference. With God's help you can work through the worst of times thus arriving at the best of times. Look at the time spend with the Darkside as a reward. An opportunity to become stronger with God by your side. TYJ

November 19

Keep your attention on the positive. If you live a life of self-guided improvement, you will alter your conditions. If you dwell on the negative upbringing by your parents, you will remain a hostage to your past. Do not allow past mistakes to take up space in your head. Learn from them. Move on for your parents came into this world with flaws. No one was born to be perfect individuals. Forgiveness will be the hardest thing you do. Many times, change means letting go of toxic people. All they do is take from you. They leave you with feelings of empty abandonment. You are not here to live up to the beliefs of others. Be who God created you to be. Learn to trust the feelings that come from deep in your soul. Do not totally believe the words of others. Watch their actions. They speak the loudest. Make the choice to stop drowning in the ocean of forlorn and despair. With morning prayer and meditation, you will find spirituality and rise above your tormenting life. The Darkside wants you to have feelings of not being enough. You can have the prettiest face, best house and the most expensive car and still have an ugly soul. You are beautiful by your acts of kindness. God loves you, flaws, and all. TYJ

November 20

Surround yourself with people you can learn from. Find God's truth. Stop worrying and put all your trust in Him. He will never tell you that you are stupid, weak, unlovable, less important than anyone else or a failure. The Darkside will suggest all of these. Learn to know which voice you are listening to. Only you can change you. It is an inside job. No one can do it for you. All I can do is pray for you. I can become your spiritual advisor, reminding you of your strengths, not your weaknesses. I can offer love and kindness that goes deep into the subconscious where all the old hurts are stored. Your part is to stay positive which will help you to create a better tomorrow. When you find yourself on a dead-end road and that feeling of emptiness enters your life, stop. Take a deep breath. Ask God to fill that empty hole in your soul with His love. Seek His guidance while traveling on your new spiritual way of life. Know that everything will work out for the best. Master the art of loving yourself enough to want to change. God will put all the broken pieces of your life together. You will see what a beautiful person you are. Love the great person you are becoming. TYJ

November 21

Part of growing up is standing up for how you feel. With morning prayer and meditation, you will improve your life. Your perception on how you view things will change. You will take on a more positive knowledge of your vague irrational beliefs. You strive for a more peaceful life. You will not let others take advantage of your emotions or dictate how you should react. You discover that you alone will make the choice on how you want to conduct your life. You master the art of dealing with your problems as soon as they happen. You no longer do things that make you feel uncomfortable. Just for today make one decision without explaining your reasoning to anyone. Turn one difficult task over to God allowing Him to carry that hardship. God will bless you with the opportunity to help you heal your brokenness. You no longer must justify your behavior. God dwells in you. He helps to keep your emotions practical. You think constructive thoughts. Be yourself. Hold your head up high letting your inner beauty shine like a beacon in the night. TYJ

November 22

Let others know how much you really care for them. That you appreciate their kindness and how they brighten your day. With morning prayer and meditation, you announce to the universe that you are blessed with God's love. He helps you to love yourself enough to make the choice to become a better person. Plant the seeds of positivity into your subconscious and watch them grow. Practice being a loving, caring person. Spend time each day doing good deeds. The action of doing will change you. Thinking of others will appear strange at first. It is humbling to look at your own faults. As you become better at helping others it will become a natural act. You will do it without thinking. By your actions, not your talk, they will know you. You reach a point in your daily routine when you just relax. Things may not turn out the way you planned. You know God has got this. He is bigger than any problem you may have today. There are options to life that do not include drugs or buying stuff. There is a Darkside waiting to drag you back into the forces of Evil. God will help you to treat anxiety, depression, rage, and loneliness. Count your blessings, choose to stay calm, listen to your soul. Be productive while performing your purpose in life of helping others. TYJ

November 23

Be cautious of the need for instant gratification. This is the time of the year to appreciate everything you have. The need to control any situation is a challenge that you cannot fulfill. You are aspiring to achieve an unattainable result on your own. You are strengthened with morning prayer and meditation. With God's help, you can mend your brokenness. Start with practicing acts of kindness and a loving soul. Let the light that is within you shine like a beacon for the darkness of others. Be an inspiration to the universe by doing what God asks you to do. Let any earthly rewards come in His time. You will know that you have learned your lesson when God quit sending you the same pain and suffering. As you trudge the past called life, learn to share your character by giving hope and understanding to others. Challenge love to its full potential for it may be all others have in today's hectic Universe. Don't be afraid to ask God for His help. He can perform miracles in otherwise hopeless situations. This is a sign of strength not weakness. You gave away your power when not facing the Truth. You will achieve self-satisfaction by doing your best. Mission accomplished. TYJ

November 24

Affirm that you are brilliant. You have the inner strength to get up each day and fight for what you believe in. you are a winner, a miracle. You are stronger because you have looked defeat in the eye and said, "NOT TODAY". By starting each day with prayer and meditation you can stop letting those negative thoughts control you. Simply say, "God, help me get through today". Pay attention to the feelings you get when you do that. You can have peace all the time. God will help you to learn from your past mistakes and keep you from repeating them. Your best days are yet to come. Thank God for all the blessings and protection He has awarded you and your family. May you show gratitude, for it is the way to happiness. Be grateful for the people who show an interest in you. Unless they show tendencies of a selfish self-centered narcissist, then run. TYJ

November 25

Today I will be satisfied with my life by my own standards. I know that remaining teachable and practicing acts of love and kindness are not a sign of weakness. They are a robust soundness of mind. My intentions are to be free from outbursts of anger today. I will practice being open to criticism without getting defensive. I strive to have no resentments towards others. I will do what my Higher Power asked me to do without fear. I will avoid the little white lies that help me to feel more important than I am. I will spend quiet time with my God as I understand Him. Morning prayer and meditation are an important part of my life. I will strive to be the best person I can be today. I no longer wallow in self-pity for my past mistakes. There are times when I need to be grateful that things did not turn out the way I wanted them to. Not everything I ruined can be fixed. I now realize they made me who I am today. I do not have anxiety for the future. That is in God's hands. I know my first purpose in life is to align myself with my Maker. There are things I cannot control. I must learn to leave them alone. I am grateful because God has blessed me with the gifts of integrity and peace of mind. TYJ

November 26

No matter how bad things get I will never give up. I need to look at my negative thinking. After writing it down, does it make sense? Is my perception accurate or fantasy? I find that a lot of my fears and negative reactions come from my childhood. I need to change my thinking from the Darkside to positive thoughts. I start each day with prayer and meditation. I tell myself that I am lovable. I am a good and worthwhile person. I will strive to be at peace with who I am today. I will not dwell on the past for my God has forgiven me for all my shortcomings. I will start today with a clean slate. I know that with God's guidance there is nothing going on in my life today that together we cannot handle. Your having a great day starts with you having positive thoughts. Be kind. Bring God's light into someone's darkness. Release any negative thoughts. Do not dwell on them. Let them go. Life is too brief to waste time on rageful outbursts or hanging on to resentments. Do not impede your blessings. TYJ

November 27

You never have to earn God's love. He has forgiven you no matter what you have done in the past. You will be required to act on those undesirable traits. Your competitive behavior will block you from the sunlight of the spirit. Our paramount shortcomings are resentments, anger, fear, and self-pity (victim). Unpleasant feelings can show up in numerous forms such as anxiety, panic or worry. God loves you so much that all you must do is ask him to remove your fears. Anger, on the other hand, will take hard work and action. You must learn to love yourself enough to want to change. Any form of resentment or anger will block you from God's good graces. Rage is basically summed up as poor impulse control. Any lack of optimism will block you from peace and serenity. Just for today treat yourself with kindness and love. Face your adversities and choose to overcome them for if you learned them, you could unlearn them. Be cautious of the Darkside. He wants you to stay emotionally unfit. Your thoughts have power. Affirm that you are a peaceful, loving person. TYJ

November 28

Do not become a director of your own negative contemplations. Remain calm. Never allow a conscious mental reaction to overpower your physiological behavior, causing you to respond with a negative outburst of arrogance. Trust me. Reacting in anger is never your best look. With morning prayer and meditation, you can shape your own positive day. Align yourself with a purpose of acquiring God's vocabulary of selflove. It is your journey. Take charge of it. It is not selfish to put your own peace and serenity first. Anyone who has suffered from depression knows how destructive it can be to any normal piece of mind. Choose to stop looking out there for your contentment. You will never find it. Living in advantageous circumstances must come from within. It starts with seeking serenity. Love yourself enough to want to practice a life without sadness or feelings of loss. Take the action to improve yourself with a happy awareness of gratitude. Stay away from selfish reflections of what you want. Everything will come in God's time. Just for today rejoice in your abilities to lead a peaceful life. TYJ

November 29

With morning prayer and meditation, you will choose to express love. Work on feeling better about yourself. You will make wiser choices. You tend not to be totally opinionated about your emotional perceptions. Do not let your fears control your negative attitudes. Know that your apprehensions display the greatest power. Anger is a maximum danger. Just for today treat yourself with love and kindness. You gain faith through the knowledge that when you turn your will and your life over to the care of God you can trust everything will work out for the best. Bad decisions from the past will still be reaping negative karma. Starting today your mission in life is to show compassion for others. Be patient, kind and gracious. Human love may fail, God's love never will. He has a solution for every problem. We tend to have an unreasonable response for every remedy. Give it to Him. Be patient some things take more time to solve than others. You did not get where you are in one day. Some took a lifetime. Be thankful for what you have accomplished so far. Prayer is the best antidote for your battles. TYJ

November 30

With morning prayer and meditation, you reach a fantastic level of freedom. You can stop worrying about what others think of you. People are going to think what they want to no matter what you do. Live your own life, not what others think you should. It is important what you think of yourself for negative in, negative out. Allow things to happen naturally so your problems can fix themselves. You can stop your controlling tendencies. May God bless you with a life of friendships. No lies. No mind games and no cheating. Do not go against the stream of life. Choose to let it run smoothly and develop on its own. Your reward will be a stress-free life. You are born with feelings for a reason. Feel them, then move on. Do not dwell on your failures. Your mind will take on a positive attitude. When the time is right, God will bless you with the fulfillment of a purpose in life. It starts with helping others. TYJ

December 1

Never underestimate the power of kindness. In every instance in your life, you are afforded the opportunity to be kind or rude. Either way, you will influence someone's life. Today, choose to love and help them. Stop letting your negative thoughts control you. If anyone makes the preference to reject you, choose to be okay with yourself. God loves you and you love yourself. Not everyone has to like you. Difficult times are not meant to destroy you. The challenges are intended to strengthen you. You know you are not perfect. There will be times when you lose your temper. You may not treat people with compassion or understanding. Stop, ask God for forgiveness and guidance. Ask His help in getting you out of the situation you got yourself into. The Darkside wants you to be angry, distressed or feeling sorry for yourself. Make your amends and vow to do better next time. Allow God to take you on the travels He had mapped out for you to fulfill your design for life. You are always responsible for what you say. You may not have an obligation on how others perceive it. TYJ

December 2

You do not have to wait for the perfect time or place to start your spiritual recovery. You can begin where you are at right now. Open the door with morning prayer and meditation. Just because life has knocked you down a few times, choose not to let sadness and failure be your norm. You will no longer allow anyone to control you or cause you to lose your inner peace. It is time to look at what you want for the New Year. May you start with giving compassion, comfort and understanding to others. Help them to find their way back to a life filled with spiritual fitness. Choose to surround yourself with a few good people who will help you to become the best possible version of yourself. Learn to take care of your mind and body be deciding on a course of action. Become a free spirit. Plant seeds of kindness. Allocate time to bond with others. See things as they are. Love the person you are today. You can achieve what you set your mind to. Start with positive affirmations. Leave the negative, broken pieces of this year behind you. Do not run from your obligation to heal yourself. Without dwelling on the past, take the time needed to feel your hurt. Stop any further difficulties. Use the help of a spiritual advisor to find your lesson. Clear away any wreckage so God can enter your life. TYJ

December 3

Stop trying to please others for you will always remain under their control. Half will say "good job" and the other half will condemn you. Tomorrow they may flip-flop. Watch how many will express complete disapproval of you for living your life for you. Start your morning with prayer and meditation, seeking God's will for you. He is the only one you really need to please 100% of the time. When going to work, know that God is the source of your income. All your good comes from Him. He uses others as instruments for your success. God is perfect love and is incapable of hate. Know that when people act with meanness or anger, they are not practicing the presence of God. They are following directions from their Darkside. Pain and suffering may mean that you are living against God's will for you. Karma also plays a role. Your biggest tragedy is to see yourself as a victim. The Darkside will do its best to keep you in that frame of mind. Set yourself free. Concentrate on what you need to do to ensure your own happiness. Come to the light. With God's inspiration take what the enemy throws at you and turn them into acts of goodness. TYJ

December 4

Whenever you feel down in the dumps with negative thoughts, work on your gratitude. Make a list of what you are grateful for. It will help to raise your level of humility. Make the choice to appreciate the little things in life. No, you cannot change all your circumstances because of bad choices you have made in the past. Through morning prayer and meditation, you know there is always something you can do to help you become a better person. By choosing to avoid conflict you will lower your level of stress and drama. Surround yourself with people who will help you with feelings of frustration from being overwhelmed. Seek a day full of God's blessings and happiness by asking Him to help you to be more loving, compassionate, and patient. Thus, lowering your chance of getting annoyed over petty things. Live without irritation during deceiving, dishonest, faithless people. Which in turn lowers your feelings of worry. You will lose the fear and uncertainty of having no control over an outcome. All this comes from one list. Try it. I guarantee you will feel better and so will everyone you meet today. Substitute your weaknesses into a constructive, confident useful attitude. Enjoy life. God only made one of you. TYJ

December 5

Life took a strange twist one day. Everything I thought I knew about my spirituality and what I wanted out of life turned to be false endeavors. What I thought was important was on the outside. In the process I lost myself to the Darkside. The more possessions I got the more I wanted. With morning prayer and meditation and following the guidelines of the prayer of St. Francis, my thinking changed. What was important was that I became who God wanted me to be. He removed my unforgiving rageful nature filled with resentments and 22 years of depression caused by being a victim. He helped me to become a kind, loving person. Life became a lot simpler when I didn't need the approval of the whole world. I am grateful for my experiences. That journey taught me how lonely and complicated life can be when I followed my will. Remove any negative thinking. Take on a program of action. Concentrate on what you want using the full power of the universe. If you are not resting on your laurels your progress will be measured by your effort. With God's help I was able to reach my purpose in life. Being a kind, loving person is priceless. All I ever needed was food, a roof over my head, sensible clothing and the love and tolerance of family and a few good friends. TYJ

December 6

Through the act of morning prayer and meditation, you are reaching out to receive the will of God for your new day. Each one will be a blessing from God. If you are free of a hostile environment. God does not live in any angry house. Choose to have God help you to remove any shortcomings that no longer serve you. He can help you to have a healthier mental attitude by improving your mindset. Doing God's will can be as simple as holding a door for someone. Give them a hello and a smile. Make the choice to not let the negativity of your past ruin your happy positive thoughts of today. You can either become better or bitter. When having completed your nightly inventory, may you see your imperfections and how brainwashed you are to the temptations of the Darkside. The action of improving will bring joy and happiness into your life. There will always be obstacles in your life so clear your mind of doubt and create a positive mental attitude. Your choice. Do not waiver from your goals. Show the Universe you can do it. TYJ

December 7

When you do morning prayer and meditation, you take on a new beauty of your inner soul and a profound happiness. You project both qualities to others. You are like a mirror reflecting your charm and grace to all those around you. The way you treat and interact with others has been altered. Your new attitude and emotional outlook on life is a miracle. Rage, bitterness, and fear have been removed and the Darkside no longer has His hold on you. You have become the person God intended you to be. There will come a time in your life when you must set boundaries to help maintain your sanity. This is not being selfish. It is called taking care of yourself. You no longer worry about how others treat you. The fundamental reason they lash out is because of the mental wounds and distress they are suffering. Your judgment becomes rational. You continue to show them love and kindness. You stop irrational, unintelligent reasons and creating problems that do not exist. The more difficult your road the bigger your rewards. Trust the process. Learn your lessons. God will never let you down. TYJ

December 8

This idea may be foreign to most of you. Be grateful for the a-holes who have made your life miserable. By hurting you the most they helped to form the strong, independent person you are today. Your part of the healing process starts with forgiving them. As badly as you may want to try to, you cannot fix them. All you can do is pray for them to want to get better. Turn them over to a God of their understanding. They may not have a Higher Power. You may be turning them over to the negative Darkside of their thinking. Everyone is born to process a strong Divine Nature. Over the years they obtained the habits of a weak, evil individual guided by their Lower Power. As bad as your pain for them may be, it is their journey, and they will have to travel it at their own speed. No one must satisfy your request. They will do it if they choose to. Everything needs to be about choice. Not, "you have to". A better way of saying it is, "it would please me if you would think of doing it this way". You on the other hand with morning prayer and meditation will learn to approach every day as a new beginning. Listen to that soft gentle voice that is telling you to let go of anger, fear and feelings of shame and guilt. Relinquish any regrets for they serve no useful benefit to anyone. Be grateful. Pass on any love and kindness you may have received today. Forward them to the next person you meet. Karma will take are of the individual who gave it to you. TYJ

December 9

I do not know how I survived the chaos and insanity of the early days of my life. With morning prayer and meditation, I now recognize the emotional and spiritual stability in my life. I recommend the loving inner peace that comes from a God-based life. My rudeness to others showed the pain I myself was living in. I was following the past of the Darkside. My mind cannot conceive both functions at the same time. Today I will choose not to ruin other people's contentment. I pray that others have a full life of wellbeing and God's blessings. I choose not to fix, judge or control anyone. Do not underestimate the power of a kind word or deed. Take the time to listen to someone else's problems. It will help to take your mind off your own. On this holiday season, make it a goal to give out more love than you receive. It will be a joyous time, your best ever. Just for today take the time to let go of one of your fears and put it in your God box. If you catch yourself taking it back, stop and re-give it to God. TYJ

December 10

By doing morning prayer and meditation, I learned one of the hardest lessons of my life. I had to let go of trying to control others and situations. Events that used to be of a paramount existence no longer had to turn out the way I perceived they should. I came to the realization that I was the problem. I became willing to work on existing to be the best person I was capable of, which is more loving and supportive. I made the choice to live life to the fullest. I gained the knowledge that I had to treat others the way I wanted to be treated. I cannot retaliate with anger and expect to receive love and kindness back. By paying attention to my rageful outburst I concluded that the Darkside was filling my mind with all the negative thoughts I was living with. I gained experience in the ability to deal with my problems by journeying deep into my soul and listen to the soft gentle voice. I made the choice to change by doing what I needed to do to make me happy. It was a hard lesson to learn I will not let what has already happened get the best of me. It had nothing to do with stuff. I became a better father, grandpa, brother, and friend to the people who were important to me. Love of myself and others was the answer to all my questions. TYJ

December 11

I made the changes in my life so I would like myself better. Once I made the choice to lead a higher quality of life, I learned to love myself and along the way others loved me. My thoughts and attitude changed and so did the people around me. I lived over half my life struggling on the Darkside but today I really enjoy being in the Light of my Higher Power who I choose to call God. Because of the miracles in my life, I grew in my knowledge that He only wanted what was best for me. I was the one who had to make the choice to believe that for He was always there waiting for me to shed my old ways. Today I know when I hit a wall to turn right. I no longer must get out my hammer and try to break through the wall. I have learned to seek God's will and to follow His plan for me. It took a lot of painful lessons to distance me from undesirable thoughts and actions. My first thought is not always my best. A major step forward was to master the art of invoking the pause in my life. It will help to reduce the amount of amends that I have to make. I had to reach constructive conclusions and stop pretending that everything was fine. My true friends will love me no matter how screwed up my day was. This holiday season try to be happy. Start with being grateful. Ask God to bless you with love and kindness. TYJ

December 12

I did not find my Higher Power who I choose to call God in any church. I like many others started out with a spiritual advisor who slowly walked me through periods of growth in which I became a better person. That spiritual teacher taught me about thinking less of myself and more of others. I found out a simple gratitude list was a shortcut to peace of mind. I now enjoy inside happiness. My spiritual counselor helps me to see how seeking help from the Universe will aid me in achieving my goals without trying to control everything. That phrase, "Let go and Let God" took on a whole new meaning. I learned that I am responsible for the effort while I turn the outcome over to God without trying to force it to end up in my favor. Acceptance became a lifesaving tool. When spending my time observing I noticed that happy people know they are the problem. They spend their time improving themselves. Unhappy, lonely people believe you are the problem and spend all their time blaming you and trying to change you. This holiday season I will work on avoiding conflict and drama. If you choose to spend time with family, try to remain calm with all circumstances. You do not have to join in the chaos. Fear is self-centered and love is God centered. TYJ

December 13

You are not meant to run from your difficulties. God wants you to work through them while learning the lessons life presents. It starts with not being ashamed or feeling guilty of who you are or what you have done. It is crucial how you judge yourself. Not other's subjective opinion of you. It will have a profound effect on your life and your survival. Pick yourself up one more time. You are constantly told to help others and to give away what was so freely given to you. Do not get lost in the needs of others and end up not taking care of yourself. Through morning prayer and meditation, you can refill your spiritual wellbeing for today's busy schedule. Taking care of yourself can be scheduling a pedicure or taking a cruise. Do not feel selfish or ashamed when expressing your wants or needs of a positive reinforcement. You do have control over your thoughts and the actions you take. Be cautious when you spend your time with toxic people for, they have a knack of causing others to drop down to their level of pain and suffering. They choose to live on the Darkside. TYJ

December 14

Today is a new day. Forget the suffering of past pain and failures. This is the first day of the rest of your life. Make the choice to make it a masterpiece. Tomorrow is not here, stop worrying about it. Choose not to let anyone get you down today. Stop fretting over what others do. They may not see things as you. You have enough friends who like the real you and accept you for what you are today. They will applaud any changes you make to become a better person. By starting your day with morning prayer and meditation you will improve your thoughts to positive and those tomorrows that you are in the state of anxiety over today. I guarantee an improvement. You will take on a less stressful mental attitude. So put on your happy face and make someone's day great by showing them love and kindness. Except what is going on in your life today. Stay strong with the good that is inside you just begging to come out. Treasure the friend who challenges you to do better. They want nothing but the best for you. They will be there through the good and bad times. Your role is to stop playing the victim. TYJ

December 15

Not everything that happens in your life is going to bring joy and happiness. Loved ones will have finished their time on Earth and will pass on. Sickness is part of our existence. Your serenity will depend upon how you handle the ups and downs of life. Acceptance and gratitude are key factors in your flow of life. Morning prayer and meditation is extremely helpful in maintaining a peaceful existence. Life will always go on. You make the choice as to how free of disturbance your existence will be during stressful times. List 5 things a day that you are grateful for. Great enjoyment comes from acknowledging the simple things in life. This will help to change your attitude. Helping others to understand how loved they are and the need to be confident human beings who value their self-worth will bring enjoyment and serenity to the both of you. Love of life will happen. It cannot be forced. No one has the right to control you. Karma is real. Clean your side of the street. Stop playing the victim. TYJ

December 16

Through prayer and meditation, you can ensure that the happiness we talked about yesterday will be part of your life today. You learn to hang with people who make you laugh. They make it easier for you to conquer your gloom and raise your spirits. Bring light into your Darkness. They lift your soul and fill that empty hole with God's grace instead of things from the outside world. The Darkside can only offer you stuff. If your soul is already filled with love and kindness be the one who assists others to fill their life with understanding. Have a passion for living by making it more acceptable for others to obtain the joy you have received in your life. Be grateful for the good graces God has bestowed on you today. Be the one who accepts others as they are. Do the best you can every day. Show them the love and kindness that they may need to make the choice to change and become a better person. Not everyone is going to appreciate what you do. Do it anyway. TYJ

December 17

A true test of your spirituality is when someone is expressing unfavorable judgement of you. Do not become defensive and angry. Look at what they are saying to see if any part of their criticism is true. Are they passing on their own low self-esteem to you instead of taking their own inventory? With morning prayer and meditation, you can check your nightly inventory and look at your own weaknesses instead of blaming others for your defects of character. Ask God to bless the other person. Not everyone is going to be joyous this time of year. Don't be the reason someone is having a bad day. It only takes a moment to be kind and loving. Though in a bit of patience. Show others your love. Just in case you were wondering, it is perfectly okay not to be perfect. Strive for excellence. Others will predict how they think you should act. Be yourself. Their projection says more about them than you. When the Darkside fears he is losing you to the light, he is going to come at you with every negative thought he can produce. Stay strong. TYJ

December 18

True prosperity is in the quality of your convictions. If you think poverty, you will continue being poor. The great law says that what you sow in your mental activities you will reap. You need to practice producing harmonious ideas. Put your house in order with righteous convictions. You can only act where your reasoning takes you. Today I will respond to blessings of gladness. Free of worries and full of God's protection. I choose to have a purpose free of selfishness, resentments, rage, malice or bitterness towards anyone. I will do my best to help others to achieve peace towards one another. I take the action to close the door to my savory past and start a new chapter in my daily routine. On page one I will choose to show love and kindness to everyone I meet today. I shall have a sense of purpose and fulfillment. I will give more thought to my day than food and clothing. Do not be a product of chance or random events. Put your process in God's hands. Be cautious of the Darkside offering you more stuff. Look for a way out of your brokenness. TYJ

December 19

Life is simple, we either learn from our misconceptions or get better. Do not allow your delusions to keep you in darkness. You will become bitter, full of rage and suffer from depression. This is not your fate in life. It is a choice. Live for today, make it a beautiful day. Do not keep making the same oversights. God puts people in your life so you can learn from them. Take the time to listen, they will teach you. Use them for they are truly sent by God. Through morning prayer and meditation, you can learn to love yourself. You will receive happiness without relying on the approval of others. You are in control of your own life. No one oversees your happiness but you. Others add to it. That is why you hang with positive, happy people. Your job is to teach others, not control them. Stay away from negative, selfish self-centered people for they have an inability to see anyone else as worthwhile. They can only pass on their own self-hatred. Their main role in life is being a martyr. You may not be able, at this time, to walk away from the selfish victim the Darkside has placed in your life. It is important to know their game. Their mentality is playing the fabrication or exaggeration of victimhood to justify their abuse on others. They have an attention seeking misconception of facts. They use circumstances against you. Their characteristic makeup is to intentionally depart from truth or accuracy. They can do no wrong. They need to face their deficiencies or end up with painful consequences in their relationships. They love to play the role of the hero or the fixer. TYJ

December 20

Tis the season to be a miracle in others lives by showing love and kindness. God chooses us to be His Angels of Good Deeds and Moral Excellence. He wants you to gain knowledge of self and Universal love of others to be kind and giving. Not everyone answers the call. The thought has been placed in your mind. You then make the choice to help or not. It is important that you stay positive starting with your own impressions. Contemplating negative opinions, like "not having enough to give to others" is putting restrictions on God's beneficial graces. When you do not give you limit God's return to you. Life is never perfect. You need to look beyond your imperfections to God's never-ending love and abundant giving. Positive awareness takes repetition. Drama is a part of your negative subconscious creation. The less you respond to it the more peaceful your life will become. Stop judging others. Focus on becoming a better person. By changing your inner beliefs, you let God increase your world around you. TYJ

December 21

As you grow in spirituality, learn to embrace what you cannot change. A byproduct of compliance is peace and happiness. Do change the one thing you can control. You. Do not wish you are someone else or seek the approval of others. Do not sweat the small stuff. Speak well of others. Work on gossip. Choose to be around positive people. Make having no resentments a goal for this New Year. One day everything will make sense and you will realize what is important in life. Be grateful for your existence today. Treat others with kindness. See problems as an opportunity for growth. Your pain has a purpose. Accept your lesson and move on. Through morning prayer and meditation, learn to love yourself enough to want to become a better person. Have faith in God that everything will work out for the best for everyone involved, not just you. May you take the opportunity this season to comprehend God in your life. Make a special attempt to focus on improving on your wrongdoings. May bliss, prosperity and love be a special gift for you this Holiday Season. TYJ

December 22

Let us not go through another holiday season carrying a resentment against another person. The first reason is it blocks you from the Sunlight of the Spirit. Second, every resentment hardens your mind and causes you bitterness, not them. Third, it causes us to receive resentments. What you sow on others you reap for yourself. It can be said in many ways. So within, so without. You create your own world. Your thoughts are contagious. A real gift to give to yourself is to settle all disputes. Forgive others, make peace and start the healing process for the good of your own sanity. There are those out there who have suffered greatly at the hands of others. Very bad karma is due to these a-holes. God cannot start to process until you let go of your hate for them. Cruel thoughts handed out by the Darkside will only bring denial and disagreement. May you make the choice to let the Peace of God enter your Soul this Festive Yuletide. TYJ

December 23

You will be meeting a lot of friends and family over the holidays. Not all of them will have your best interest in mind. Accept things for the quality they are. Not what your opinion is on what they should be. Situations happen for a reason. You do not always get all that you desire. Sometimes God says no to your prayers. He always has your best interest in mind. If He closes a door stop trying to get in through a window. Look at the bright side, everything will be fine, enjoy yourself. Get excited, stop fearing that the worst is going to happen. Expect the best. Your temptations become your assumptions and your insecurities become your actions. Start your ideas with happiness and joy through morning prayer and meditation. Become aware of your anxieties. Learn to successfully navigate through them without falling to the Darkside's enticement to seduce you with stuff you can't afford at this time. You cannot control what others are going to conceive in their mind or do. Let it go. Spend as much time as you can with your positive family and friends. TYJ

December 24

This is not the time to isolate. Have a plan to be with people who are good for your spirituality. If you made the choice to turn your will and your life over to God, then trust His plan for this holiday season. He will always be there for you when others fail. If the possibility arises that you may not remain calm, stop, hit the pause button. Try, learn, forgive, take a break. Choose to remain peaceful no matter what is going on. Teach others to treat you with respect. Stay strong in your faith. Do not let the worry of not having the finances to spread all the joy you wanted to get you down. To your true friends and family your presence in their lives will be more than any gift you could buy them. Offer to help others for it is all about the giving, not the receiving. Do not let your expectations of others ruin your holiday fun. It will be a losing battle if you let your emotions get the best of you. Do not waste time feeling sorry for yourself if this Christmas is not working out the way you hoped for. Let it go. Controlling others is not the answer. Work on becoming a better person. Make the choice to have fun. TYJ

December 25

I am wishing all my morning prayer and meditation friends and family a Merry Christmas. To me, you are all priceless and irreplaceable. Our trying experiences have been phenomenal and utmost worthwhile part of my passage into my Spirituality God guided improvement. Today I choose to have positive people in my life. I will not judge anyone or play the victim role. I want my Karma to be joyous. I appreciate and respect every one of you. I love to spend my time with people whose passion is to laugh and have fun. I feel cherished when I am around you. May you all be filled with God's deep affection and kindness today. If you are carrying a heavy load in your life, may it be lightened and may your Christmas be filled with happiness and joy. Nothing in the outside world can compare to God's supreme prosperity and success when you choose to walk with Him. Seeking God's approval ensures your acceptance to be a peaceful voyage through any roadblocks the Darkside may have tried to exploit. TYJ

December 26

If you have not learned anything else through this holiday season, be who you are. No one can replace you. If others don't like it remember your happiness is not contingent on pleasing others. It is about taking care of yourself without being selfish. Yesterday represented one day in your existence, it is not your whole journey. Your spiritual growth is a byproduct of having peace, love and joy in your Soul. Not everyone is meant to be in your functional activities forever. Their part was to teach you the lesson you needed to learn. To improve your growth. Now it is time for them to move on. You can lower your anxiety level by not trying to control the future. If you want to alter your existence, take action to adjust your reasoning. So, let's get ready to make this coming New Year the best ever. Start with believing in yourself. TYJ

December 27

It is time to act on how you are going to make this New Year your best ever. You must begin with your thoughts. Believe you are a worthwhile person. Work on your goals to become a better person. Dream big. Keep your head where your feet are. Put your own wellbeing first. Do not worry about what others think. Know that people pleasing is not an asset. Treat others with respect, the same way you want to be treated. Join positive groups. They will help you find the courage to change and give you the strength to follow your visions. They will assist you on maintaining your faith in God while supporting you on becoming a caring, loving soul. Let those who treated you badly in the past know that you will no longer accept bad behavior on their part. As you grow in your spirituality you will find that you do not fit in with everyone. Look for the good in any negative encounter you meet today. Do not get angry or resentful. Reflect on how you will be better prepared for your next confrontation. You are responsible for your own happiness. Do not make the mistake of thinking that if you look good on the outside everything is fine. If your insides are ugly, you are an ugly person. No one can ever do enough to make you happy. It must come from the inside. The Darkside can only offer you stuff. Stop playing the role of a victim. TYJ

December 28

In order to make the changes you want for the New Year you will have to take some action. It means getting off the couch and making the choice to become a different person. That soft gentle voice will tell you to keep going. You got this. Learn to make the decisions that are best suited for your life. Live in peace with your fellow human beings in a spiritual way. Choose to make your story the best ever. Select to show compassion for your fellow human beings. Decide to act with kindness and integrity and to conduct yourself with respect and humility. Life will go on whether you choose to take the action to get better or not. Things may not always work out for the best. At least you can say you gave it your best. One thing you know for sure is that if you choose to stay on the couch your life will only get worse. Prefer to create a positive mental attitude. Clear your mind of self-doubt. Show the world you can do it. When you feel drained, ask God to calm your anxieties and to take your fears away. God lets you know how blessed you are to be alive and healthy. If He affords you the opportunity to help someone, do it. TYJ

December 29

For this coming New Year make the choice to change. It starts with loving yourself enough to want to recover from your soul sickness. First, you will have to take the initiative to work on unconditional love for yourself. It will take discipline to make the transition to self-care. Second, getting up early enough to do the morning prayer and meditation. It is imperative that you have some sort of Higher Power in your spiritual existence. You may need to start with a spiritual advisor and work towards a God of your understanding. This will help to alleviate fear and anxiety by turning your concerns over to a Power greater than yourself. You cannot do this alone. You are gong to have your ups and downs. There will be days when past hurts are going to come back. Healing is difficult. Get grounded, make the phone call and stay in touch with your spiritual advisor. They only want what's best for you. You must accept that you are worthy. May your Higher Power bless your soul with whatever your desires are for the New Year. If nothing changes, there is no prospect of altering your Spiritual development. Stop playing the victim role. TYJ

December 30

Your happiness for the New Year will depend upon how you view your present situation. What you have done in the past is ancient history. You can make your future brighter by doing good today. This is the only day you are responsible for. Stop complaining about your problems and be grateful for what you have. You have grown for God has wrapped you in His endless Grace. Be thankful for the good. God is saying to you that things will work out in His perfect timing. Take the time to see how you have learned from your past mistakes. Enjoy living in peace, not drama. Do not let the Darkside convince you that your life is a useless mess. Constructive optimistic results come from positive thoughts. Those will come from God. Stay in today. Your thoughts are powerful. Do not think any negativity about yourself. Your thoughts made you who you are. Know the difference. He will never tell you to throw a brick through someone's window. God wants you to have stuff. It will happen after you have chosen Him as your Higher Power. TYJ

December 31

As you close out the old year look back at your life today. Be grateful that God gave you a second chance at life. He has brought you from a world of addictions filled with shame, disgrace, sorrow and failure to a life of positive results while living in His glory. Are you gong to start the New Year with a place to live, food on the table and clothes to wear? You have people who care for you. These are the things you need to be thankful for. You are not perfect. You never will be. Bloom where you are planted. Be who you are. You need to give yourself credit that you made the choice to fight your demons and follow God's plan and purpose for you. It includes being happy, helping others and doing what is right. Not everyone you will meet today will have accomplished what you have learned. They may still be struggling with negative feelings. Your part is to show them kindness for they are an emotionally sick person. Tell them not to give up. Miracles do happen and God can and will change things. Being a prisoner to things you cannot change is a storm you need to avoid. Never lose your enthusiasm for life. By starting your day with morning prayer and meditation you can spend as much time dressing up your insides as you do your outsides. Believe that good is going to happen. Fill your life with Grace and gratitude. TYJ

www.ingramcontent.com/pod-product-compliance
Lightning Source LLC
Chambersburg PA
CBHW032031150426
43194CB00006B/231